OVER(
ADVE

C000172997

OVERCOMING ADVERSITY

HELEN MCMENAMIN-SMITH

To
Barbel

Very best Wishes
Helen x

StoryTerrace®

Text Julie Abrams-Humphries, on behalf of Story Terrace

Design Grade Design & Adeline Media, London

Copyright © Helen McMenamin-Smith

Text is private and confidential

First print October 2018

StoryTerrace·

www.StoryTerrace.com

ACKNOWLEDGEMENTS

First, I would like to say a huge thank you to all those who saved my life. Starting at the roadside with Alan Chapman, Chris and Nikki Pearson, the MAGPAS team, the paramedics and emergency crews.

At the hospital, the surgeons, doctors, nurses, the whole medical team of NCCU at Addenbrookes, and the dedicated work of the Addenbrookes Rehabilitation Unit, the ECHIS team and Headway.

I would like to thank my husband, John and my daughter, Alyx for the love and the care they gave me for the difficult years after the accident and my prolonged recovery.

In earlier years, I am indebted to my work colleagues who were so helpful and inspirational, Colin Hardy, Duncan Rhead, Glynn Hall, Ian Bucklow, Norman Stockham, Alan Cousens, Chris Fowler and Paul Lester.

I am writing this book because I have had a very different life. At times very difficult, at times very successful, at times very sad and at times very lucky. Throughout this book you will see that although life has often been hard, I never gave up hope. I fought many battles and came through successfully.

My last major battle started on 25th of May 2013 and I am extremely lucky to still be alive and to be able to walk, talk, read and write. Because of this I thought my story might make interesting reading. Throughout life don't expect things to be handed to you on a plate, learning, working hard and having good communication skills are so important. Even if you can't go to university there will still be a route to a successful life. Don't worry about the environment you are in, I started my career in a man's world and never looked back. I had a fantastic and very successful working life which ended with another situation to overcome.

Sales of this book will contribute to raising funds for MAGPAS, the air ambulance charity which saved my life. Some of the UK's expert doctors and paramedics volunteer their own time to work with MAGPAS, the air ambulance is not a state-funded service and relies on generous public donations to continue saving lives.

CONTENTS

1

BRITTLE FRACTURES

A hospital orderly placed the plastic tray on the trolley above my bed and left. I couldn't be sure he was a hospital orderly. I left that to the frazzled connections in my brain, relying on the link between his uniform and the white walls of the room, to make the deduction that meant I was in a hospital, in a quiet, empty room. The strings and tubes of drugs, bloods, electrolytes, drips and pouches had been taken away before I even knew they were there. Silent monitors guarded my bedside, their functions reduced from urgent to routine. All I had left to describe to me what had happened were the scars, the angry, jagged marks across my skin. I looked down at the plastic tray, a compartmented assortment of grey hospital food and thought, *What has he left that for? What am I meant to do with it?* I was incapacitated by a mind that had erased my trauma as if re-booting a computer – 'control, alt, delete' – it had turned off my memory without turning it on again.

Memory is a trickster. You think you have it, your story, but it is a lie hiding in the truth. I have absolutely no recall of the 25th May 2013, in fact I have a complete memory blank of the subsequent 40 days. It is mostly through the witness from professionals, friends and family, and the complete strangers who saved my life that I can re-construct that day, the rest falls into a dark chasm, a yawning gap that has been filled by the memories of others. My memory shut down, protecting the brittle fractures in my brain.

I know that in some ways, the third week in May of 2013 was a hopeful and optimistic one for my family, a period when we were all looking forward to the future. After six months, my husband John was firmly settled into retirement, our daughter, Alyx, was happy at school, working for her GCSE's, and predicted to do well. My chronic lupus was being managed and, like a shark that must keep swimming or expire, I had been proactive in doing things for others and learning new skills for myself. One of which had been booking a photography day course in Hunstanton with my friend Jill, arranged through another friend, Phil Mynot. There would be another eight people attending. Jill was a nurse at Addenbrookes Hospital in Cambridge and shared my passion for photography. I'd packed all my equipment, a Canon 7D DSLR camera with several different lenses, and my tripod. I thought I looked quite the professional. Jill and I laughed when we had arrived at the hotel the night before, they had allocated us a ground floor room with an adapted bathroom for the disabled.

"Perhaps they thought I was your older, much, much older sister." I joked, not knowing what a portent the bathroom would be.

I know I was happy that day in Hunstanton, a quiet seaside town on the North Norfolk Coast with carrot cake cliffs, a wide sweep of sea and gentle greens that soften the edge of the eroded land. In late May, the sea is glass green and opaque and sunlight flickers on the moving water. Standing on the sand with the others, I raised my camera, adjusted the shutter speed and took some shots of the sea. It was warm and dry, and the sea breezes stirred our clothes as we walked along the wide sweep of beach. We took lunch in one of the cafés on the front, chatting and laughing, before going back to the shingle beach and photographing until our shadows stretched in the late afternoon sun. Those photographs would capture my last memories. Pictures lost in the fire, swiped clean.

At around 3 p.m., I packed up my photography equipment and, putting Jill's bag in the back of my VW Tiguan, left the hotel in preparation for the journey home. It was a Saturday and I'd left enough time to negotiate the weekend traffic. I planned to get home by five. John had promised to cook a good dinner, a roast with all the trimmings, one of my favourite meals. I don't like it very much now. I put our luggage in the boot of the car. Jill slid into the passenger seat, seatbelt clicked into place for safety, her profile lit by the late afternoon sun. I glanced in the rear-view mirror. My reflection looked back at me calmly, neat hair and bright, blue eyes. I knew who I was;

the driver, the responsible, capable, organised one. I started the engine and pulled out of the car park. That is the last memory I have of that day.

We drove back along the A10 towards Ely. Knowing there would be Saturday traffic building up around the city centre, I took a quieter route along Branch Bank at Littleport, alongside the river Lark, a tributary of the Ouse. From the air, the landscape there looks like an intricate computer circuit board, grids of rivers divide flat farming fields bisected by long roads. We drove along lanes edged by green fields, frilled with foaming cow parsley and scatters of white hawthorn blossom. As we rounded a stretch by The Swan pub we noticed some well-spaced traffic behind, and little traffic ahead. A clutch of cars and some motorbikes passed us on the opposite side of the road. The motorcyclists were a group of friends who had been out for the day. One had fallen behind. 24 years old and now riding a new, more powerful bike his grandfather had recently bought him, he chose that moment to exercise its power and twisted the throttle in a fast and furious acceleration, speeding down the road to catch up with the others. Through inexperience, he completely lost control of the powerful bike and careered towards the driver's side of my white Tiguan like a nail to a magnet. I'm told I did everything I could to avoid the collision. I would have braked, I would have tried to swerve. There was no time. His bike completely crushed the front of the car (thank god for crumple zones) and doused it in petrol. He was now a human projectile and hit the roof just above my head. I was thrown forward and my head smashed into the impacted metal depression in the roof. The motorbike rider was killed instantly. My Tiguan rolled onto its roof and burst into flames. Jill dragged herself from the car, screaming. My seatbelt locked in place and hung me upside down, my scalp had been virtually removed and I was bleeding severely, internal damage to my brain had begun. The initial impact broke millions of neural connections, the internal bleeding was increasing pressure in my skull, damaging more and more of these precious connections second by second.

Back along the road, traffic stopped and started to build up. Alan Chapman was on his way to Soham to visit some friends. When he saw my mangled car and realised there was someone trapped inside, he raced along the road to the scene, crawled under the smouldering wreckage and, remarkably, managed to release the seatbelt undeterred by the singe of his own clothes and flesh, smoking in the evening light. Five cars further back were off duty RAF Flight Lieutenants Chris Pearson and Trainee Medical Officer Nikki Harrison who were on their way for an evening meal at a nearby pub with Nikki's parents. Chris and Nikki left their guests in the car and ran forward into the billowing smoke. Chris helped Alan pull me clear, fearing an imminent fireball they carried me to the other side of the road, as far away from the car as they could. Minutes later the car exploded into flames. Nikki joined Chris and Alan at the roadside and showed them how to keep my neck still. She was one of the first to save my life that day.

I was a horrific sight, a small, mashed up woman who was beginning to choke on her own blood. She turned me on my side to stop that happening and, when I stopped breathing, she gave me CPR, pumping my chest in rapid beats while someone called an ambulance. As I gasped for breath, the trio kept me warm and stopped my body from going into shock. All three had risked their lives without thought or hesitation to help a stranger.

Jill did go into shock, she must have felt as though she had been dropped onto the set of a disaster movie, watching events unfold as if she wasn't there. Traumatised, she froze, and could only watch as other, stunned drivers did, too shocked to know what to do. I didn't hear the sirens and the screaming fire engines that were soon on the scene, I couldn't smell the burning of flesh and metal. The paramedics took one look at me and knew it was too dangerous, and would take too long, to move me by road to a hospital. They called in the air ambulance. I could not hear the clatter of the rotor blades against the bright blue East Anglian sky as MAGPAS Heli Medix arrived, with another person who would save my life that day, Dr Wayne Kark. When the air ambulance landed, he ran over to me and resuscitated me again, twice. It was clear from the extent of my head injuries that brain damage was a critical issue. In such cases, time is of the essence. He put me into a medically induced coma to reduce the swelling in my brain and start taking control of all my vital functions. I was loaded into the air ambulance and they flew me to

Addenbrookes Hospital where I was admitted to Accident and Emergency just one hour after impact. Only later would I understand just how critical that was. The fact that the air ambulance, MAGPAS, is effectively a mobile A&E unit meant that medical intervention could start at the roadside and the critical process of limiting the extent of further brain injury was underway only yards away from my burnt-out vehicle.

2

LOOSE CONNECTIONS

18 months later I am sat in our house in Burwell, on Silver Street, watching the late afternoon news. Janine Machin is poised behind a swish BBC desks in the studio in Norwich, wearing a green jacket with a remembrance poppy in her lapel. The large screen behind her, a frozen VT image of my mangled, inverted Tiguan with a picture of a clutch of paramedics around a stretcher above it, my body hidden by their high vis jackets. It's a few minutes of news on the local bulletin, but all my life before and after. Graphics tumble, forming into a word, 'RESCUE' in huge, red font as the reporter begins her voice over:

"The driver of the car was trapped inside, sustaining life threatening injuries. A year and a half later, Helen McMenamin-Smith is back on her feet, and today she returned to thank the passers-by and the medics who saved her."

The screen switches from the still image of my mangled Tiguan, to film. There I am, wearing an angelic white crew neck, my daughter Alyx is to my left in a smart grey polo and my husband John across the table in a check shirt and blue jumper. We are sat around a table, clutching disposable coffee cups, pretending to chat over slices of cake as the reporter continues, "It's a moment this family never thought they would have, chatting together 17 months after mum, Helen, nearly died. She'd been involved in a horrific crash on a Fenland Road near Ely. A motorcyclist was killed while Helen's car span out of control."

The footage cuts to me, I look off camera, doubtful, my right eye is off at a tangent, my fringe covers the ladder of scars on my head. Here my memory lies, I still remember nothing after packing the car with my camera equipment. I'm re-telling what I have been told, as if I could remember. I'm speaking, automatically, "The car rolled over and landed upside down, so I already had terrible head injuries, then the car caught fire, but amazingly there were passers-by who were willing and brave enough to help me."

That is the indisputable truth, I think, as I continue to watch the report. Cut to myself and a MAGPAS pilot chatting outside the helicopter, Chris and Alan are behind me, shadowed by the huge rotors we look like we're on a school trip.

The voiceover continues, "Those passers-by were Alan, who pulled Helen to safety, with Chris and partner Nikki, both serving at RAF Marham. All three reacted instinctively."

Cut to Chris, an impressive tag line rolls across the screen below his headshot: 'Chris Pearson – tornado navigator – RAF Marham, flight lieutenant.'

"There were a few spectators who weren't really doing anything, and we soon discovered that Helen was still in the car and the front of the car was on fire. The adrenaline really took over and we just tried to get her out of the car as quickly as possible."

A photograph interrupts his narrative. It's me, laid out on a white pillow, my head tilted to one side, right eye closed and a red welt of stitches across my forehead. My head looks like a boiled egg that someone has sliced the top off and then replaced, or a still from an early *House of Hammer Horror*. Watching, I wince. The reporter continues, "Helen had severe head and spinal injuries and the trio battled to keep her alive until doctors from MAGPAS arrived," and we're back to the picture of my body, hidden by at least seven fire, paramedic and ambulance people, there are boxes of medical supplies open all over the ground, including a canister of oxygen. Someone has erected a green fabric screen, shielding me from public view.

There are tubes everywhere, "Among them Wayne Kark," the film cuts to a shot of Wayne looking earnestly at a computer screen in his office, I walk in wearing my white sweater, arms outstretched ready for an embrace. We hug, I talk into his back as the camera creeps in for a close-up, "who put Helen into a medically induced coma, she was then flown to hospital. Today Helen met Wayne for the first time since the crash."

It's Wayne's turn for a headshot to camera, "We treat a lot of patients, but we rarely get to see the outcome of what happens, so to get to see Helen, who when I first met her was essentially unconscious and will have no recollection of what happened at the time, it's amazing." That's the truth, shining out from the television screen, bright as a diamond.

I reinforce his words in my headshot to camera, "I'm just amazed, every day I'm grateful now that I'm still here as the head injuries were so, so very severe." The film loops back to our little group, posing for a photo in front of the tail of the air ambulance, on which are emblazoned the words, 'Support us and save a life.' The reporter finishes her piece, "Helen still has some difficulties but she's planning to get back on the road in the new year." I did. I kept going. The accident was life-changing but I don't remember the moment it changed my life. I'm retelling things I know to be true, because others have told me, I've seen the evidence.

I don't remember the flight in the air ambulance on the 25th May, I don't remember being rushed through A&E to be surrounded by expert staff, and the operations by Mr Hutchinson's team. A consultant neurologist who specialised in neurotrauma and head injury, he had been consulted as an expert after the racing driver, Michael Schumacher had suffered a horrific injury in a skiing accident. These people kept me alive.

Meanwhile, John was at home preparing that roast dinner, oblivious to the drama. He was getting a little riled because the roast dinner was nearly ready, and I wasn't home, it was on the verge of spoiling, so he called Jill's house to see if I was there. Jill's husband Anthony answered, and John said, "Where have the girls got to?"

"Jill is still at the scene of the accident and Helen is on her way to Addenbrookes in the air ambulance." He answered. John had no idea what he was talking about. He was shocked and confused. Anthony said he would come over immediately. Shortly afterwards there was a knock at the door, John was expecting Anthony, but when he opened the door there were two policemen standing there, hats in hands. They informed him that I had been in a very serious accident and that he should get to Addenbrookes hospital as soon as possible. Anthony then arrived and drove them both to the hospital. The nurses in A&E told John to wait in a cubicle and that someone would come and speak to him soon. He was not taken to the family room. We did not know at the time, but the family of the deceased motorcyclist were in there. John waited for over an hour, but still no one came. Eventually the two policemen who had come to the house wandered past and saw him, amazed that he was still there and not with a professional or had been taken to see me. There was a lot going on in A&E that night and the consultant who was meant to speak to him had been called to another emergency. The policemen soon made sure someone spoke to John.

The first 24 hours after a severe head injury are critical. The medical team could not give John a hopeful forecast. I had a 50% chance of survival and was still in a coma. He did not know what his wife would wake up to be, or if she would wake up. Over the next days and months, our lives moved from one level of uncertainty to the next. A trauma stops time, and when it starts again, it edges forward slowly, like a snail on a greased pole. Increments of progress are measured by survival, tiny steps on a staircase of increasing uncertainty and anxiety.

I was in intensive care for 22 days and in rehab for a further 40 days. In ITU they tried to raise me from the coma several times, but each time my cranial pressure became critical and my vital signs were deteriorating, so they put me back in. After the first week my cranial pressure was more stable but when the sedation and respirator was removed I was unable to breathe for myself. At the end of day 22 in intensive care they took me off the respirator. I couldn't swallow and had lost all automatic muscle function and had to be tube fed. They moved me over to the rehab ward and the long, slow process of recovery began. 40 days after the accident I emerged from a period of which I have no recollection and looked at the person sitting next to my bed with puzzlement. I did not recognise John, I had no idea who he was and didn't understand why I was in hospital. My mind was lost in a sea of nothing, until, slowly, small islands of memory returned. Isolated islands like a scattered atoll, islands grown with tangled trees of bewildered wood. It became not a question of, "Who are you?" any more, but more a question of "I think I know who you are, have I got it right?" Eventually bridges formed between these islands and I started to build back my memory. John made me a chronological family album, we started at page one and worked through it together many times. He showed me who my parents were, my family, daughter and who he was. Only close family and friends could visit, including my surviving brother, Paul, and his wife, Beverly. Slowly I began to remember who these people were.

I had no memory of the accident, John had to tell me what had happened. Jill's husband Anthony, who worked as a theatre manager at Addenbrookes, visited him for support as both their wives had been through the same trauma. Later on, in my recovery, Jill came to see me with another friend, Amanda. We walked down to the Costa Coffee in Addenbrookes, I remembered I liked coffee. The accident changed so many of our lives, Jill remembered everything about it and was so traumatised that she suffered severe depression afterwards. Seeing me triggered all her memories and so some time later I convinced Jill that it would be better if we did not see each other for a while.

Throughout it all John kept a daily diary. He wrote down treatments, progress, his emotions and reactions. It proved cathartic for him to do this and gave him a coping mechanism. It also gave him enough information to put together a daily email bulletin, that he sent out to family and friends at 10 p.m. every night. It stopped the constant phone calls and offers of help, given with the best intentions. It had been hard for him to repeat the same information over and over. He was by my side every day. Alyx was just about to start her GCSE's and the school said she could defer, but, like her mother, she's a determined girl and didn't want to put them off. Despite enormous pressure, she completed them and got fantastic results, eight A's and two B's.

My physical recovery was slow. I was bed bound for so long, the first time I was allowed out of bed and able to shower myself, it felt like a huge achievement, I behaved as if I had won the Olympic medal for showering, ecstatic to feel warm water on my skin, to feel clean and in control of my body for just that short time. When I was able to walk, the nurses helped me down to a special garden on the ward. They had allowed one of my little Parson Jack Russells to be brought in. I recognised Barney immediately and of course, he knew me. I was overjoyed.

Two days before the accident I had been visiting my Uncle John at his home after he was discharged from Addenbrookes with a heart problem. I promised I would visit him again after the Hunstanton photography course. Uncle John was such an important person in my life and had helped me so much as a child and young adult. We were great friends who often went on photography courses together. My brother had called me during my photography course and told me Uncle John had been rushed back into hospital, my intention was to see him the next morning. He was in a nearby ward when I was flown in. As I fought for my life, he lost his battle and died two days after I was admitted. One death in a family comes so close to one life given. I knew I owed him so much. I owed it to him, my family, my rescuers and myself to recover from this catastrophe and live a good life. Every time I think of Uncle John, I know that he would be very pleased to see my progress.

Throughout my stay, the medical and rehab team at Addenbrookes were amazing. My consultant neurologist, Judith Allanson still checks up on me, even now, to ensure that everything is going well, as I have had a few scary moments even after four years. One piece of good advice that Judith gave me was: "Helen, you need to be Mrs Sensible more and stop doing so much." I totally agreed. A few years after the accident I was able to give a couple of talks for her, both related to brain injury. Finally, they could do no more in hospital and it was time for me to go home.

3

I RISE - RECOVERY

They let me go home for two nights. When I emerged from Addenbrookes, the world felt as overwhelming to me as new life to a baby. We drove back to our house in Burwell, but it felt alien and frightening. I was so unsettled, I wanted to go back into hospital where I felt safe and my surroundings were familiar. I was so traumatised during my first night at home, I went back into hospital the next morning. John was infinitely patient with me and reassured me all would be well, he was likely thinking anything but. While I was in hospital his brother had said to him, "You'll need to build a toilet downstairs and do something about that gravel outside." The house was an obstacle course, everything became a trip hazard or a danger. It was like child proofing the house all over again, but this time for an adult. Adapted equipment was provided, raised toilet seats for the bathrooms so I did not have far to lower my weak body, stools and rails brought in. If I had had the mental capacity to notice the similarity to the hotel bathroom the day before my accident, I would have laughed at the irony.

John became my carer and the balance in our relationship switched. We had to take everything day by day. Caring goes on for months and years and is exhausting for close family. I became completely dependent on other people for such a long time. This had never been the case. I'd always been independent and had looked after myself since I was a small child. Rehab and professional support were provided. ECHIS (Evelyn Community Head Injury Service) sent specialist therapists to the house, following up the physio and assessments I had in hospital. I had weekly one-to-one sessions with a psychiatrist for post-traumatic stress disorder, until I joined a support group at ECHIS. At first this was very frightening and I would not speak, but it helped to listen to others with similar experiences. Seeing the struggles the others in the group had to overcome was inspiring. I thought, *If they can do it, so can I*. They gave me the strength to keep going. The carers and therapists were brilliant. They also provided support sessions for John as well, which he found extremely beneficial, as it was a recovery process for him too.

At home I spent all my time laid in bed or on the settee, oblivious to the summer passing in my garden, the buzz of bees in the hollyhocks and the hum of nearby lawnmowers. My mind had entered stasis, there was little I could concentrate on. I couldn't watch TV or read, I had lost the words to name things, so John had to help me every day and used the iPad to show me pictures with labels, so I could relearn what things were, but I could only focus for a few minutes at a time.

I didn't even know how to use the TV remote. I had to re-learn all my fine motor skills. I had to learn to use the computer again and, although I had always been brilliant at spelling, it deteriorated significantly.

I told myself I had been lucky, incredibly so. Sometimes that worked, it was true. I didn't want to allow myself to get too down or depressed as I was lucky to be alive. I never thought, *I've had enough of this.* I never gave in to despair, although I came close and there were plenty of tears when I did. I was an invalid for at least a year. I was improving very slowly, stepping forward day-by-day with tiny steps on a long, winding road to recovery. The therapy and medication helped me cope, the little white pills of Citalopram became my sword against the onset of fear, combined with the excellent support groups and career and family I had around me. I had always tried to look on the positive side. What happened was horrible and traumatic, but it happened, I had to move thorough it.

I longed to be outside and feel the fresh air on my face and there are some beautiful places near where I live. It was so important to my recovery to get out of the house and walk. That first proper walk was in March 2016, over two years after the accident. When I felt brave enough, I persuaded John to walk me down to the little river that runs nearby. A walk through our pretty village with its pastel coloured cottages, neat grass verges and corner shop, over a small bridge to the river where swans glide and narrowboats park. When we finally got there, my heart sank at the sight. Rubbish littered the banks and choked the undergrowth, floating on the green water. I was very disappointed. I asked John if he would go back with me, armed with plastic bags and rubber gloves, and pick it all up. I felt personally offended, how could people treat the place like that? Because of what had happened to me, I was so in awe of natural beauty in the world, I couldn't understand that others would not feel the same way, that they could not appreciate something so precious and beautiful. A couple of months later and feeling a bit stronger, I asked John if he would drive me to the Devil's Dyke car park at the other end of Burwell, so that we could have a walk along this beautiful ancient path. Devil's Dyke is the largest of several earthworks in South Cambridgeshire, that were designed to control movement along the ancient Roman roads. When we arrived, I was horrified at the amount of litter and some fly tipping refuse. My indignation gave me a cause and a new drive, and something to occupy my mind. I took photos of all the rubbish and then John and I cleared it up and left the bags to be collected. I then took another photo of our miraculous work. I was now able to use the computer again, so I wrote about my experience on the Burwell residents' Facebook page and posted my photos. I soon discovered that a lot of the villagers felt the same way and so appreciated what John and I had done. I took their comments and my opinions to a Parish council meeting one evening and asked them if they would support me to start a 'Litter Picking' group. If they were able to give me a budget of £200 I could buy 12 new sticks and

30 tabards to wear. One night I held a meeting at the council office and Paul Webb and Pete Lancaster helped me to decide what our group should be called so that we could have it printed on our Tabards. It was BCCC - Burwell Community Clean-up Campaign. It is still running very successfully, and we have taken on other projects as well, but most importantly John and I have made some very good friends. I also became brave enough to re-join the Bottisham and Burwell Photo Club, re-learning the competence and creativity I had lost in the accident. As I was not yet driving, two very good friends from the photography club used to pick me up and drop me off every Tuesday evening. Thank you, Daphne and Barry. I also re-joined my French group too and tried to re-learn the language. Before the accident my French fluency was very good, I used the language a lot because we loved going to France in our motorhome. After the accident, I had fallen so far behind my French group friends. I felt I was not good enough and would hold them back, so I was going to leave, but they persuaded me to stay.

It took a further three years before I felt like I was returning to any semblance of normality. After two years I had started going to Headway's gym, Headway is another group specifically set up for people with Brain Injuries. At each one-hour session, one coach was responsible for three patients, I was one of them. Veer, our Instructor, was amazing. When I first went I could only sit on a bike and pedal for a short time. Two years later I was running on the treadmill for 20 minutes and using all the other special equipment easily.

My life became a list of therapy and hospital appointments. The routine would help to structure my week and give me daily motivation. On my busiest day there was gym at Headway at 1 p.m., with hydro pool at two fifteen, John picking me up and dropping me off in between. It was the most difficult day, as I usually went for a rest at 2 p.m., but the timetable prevented that. I made good friends at these sessions though and after four years I started to think I could do some of the therapy on my own and went back to mainstream gyms and pools.

A year after I left hospital, and after many visits to the Eye Clinic at Addenbrooks, I went back in for an operation on my eye. It was now looking the right way, but I had double vision. Glasses that blanked one eye helped with this, but I hated wearing them. Thankfully the surgeons partially corrected this, but I still have a problem when I look up or down.

I felt so lucky that I had such great teams of people in so many places who helped me on my road to recovery that I wanted to give something back. I gave interviews to the local press and national magazines on the accident and recovery and donated the fee to MAGPAS, raising awareness of how they are funded and what support they need.

I stayed in touch with everyone who helped me at the accident. My debt to them is endless. Chris and Nikki are now married and have a lovely little girl. At one time John, Alyx and I visited Chris at RAF Marham. He showed us so many interesting things including what they wear when they are flying which looked very uncomfortable. We took a picture of me sitting in the cockpit of a tornado, Chris at my side. When he opened the engine of the Tornado he navigates, I was amazed and fascinated to see there were Microcircuits made by MCE (Micro Circuit Engineering) the company I used to manage. A little of my life history had been flying with him before we met on that roadside.

Overturned Tiguan

Wayne Kark and paramedics

Head injury post-surgery

Myself with Wayne, Chris and Alan, the people who saved my life, and John and Alyx, who helped me rebuild it

Alan and me

Reunion with Nikki, me, John and Chris

4

BUILDING FOUNDATIONS - EARLY LIFE

I was born on the 11th June 1962 in Dunstable hospital, Bedfordshire. The National Health Service was still in its teens. In America, Kennedy was embroiled in the Cuban missile crisis and Monroe had died. Back in Britain, Cliff Richard was the golden boy of British pop with a little-known Liverpool band making their first chart appearance behind him. That winter was going to be one of the coldest on record, but June in Dunstable was balmy. My mother was delighted to have a baby girl on her third attempt, I had two older brothers, David and Paul, waiting at home.

My mother was Valerie McMenamin, nee Mandeville. She was Sawston born and bred from an established Cambridgeshire family, the daughter of Roy Eversden Mandeville and Edith Mirey Horsnell. Mandeville is an auspicious surname that crops up throughout British history, French in origin, coming into England after the Norman conquest, when Geoffrey de Mandeville was granted large estates at Walden in Essex.

Roy Eversden Mandeville, my grandad, did well for himself too. He ran a successful lorry business and they lived in a large Victorian house on Hillside, Sawston. Not quite an estate, but he ran it like one.

It had generous lawns and a big back garden. Grandad had one of his brick-built garages at the house converted into a betting shop, he ran that business successfully from home. He would go to work in a three-piece suit and when he came home at the end of the day, remove his jacket and hang it over his spade, roll up his sleeves and set to work in his garden, still wearing his waistcoat.

Their daughter Valerie was an independent spirit, vivacious with her auburn curls styled short and always wore a stylish pair of glasses. She was an attractive woman attracted to men, something that did not fade with age. It caused rifts between us in later life, although she remained my best friend and supported me in her own way. Valerie was born in 1936, she was 16 years younger than my dad. They met when she was working as a telephone operator in Sawston. She would listen to his phone calls while she operated the exchange. Taking a liking to his soft Irish brogue, and impressed by his conversations, my mother engineered a meeting between them. My father was captivated by her charms and they fell in love. They were married in early 1956. She was 20, a bride in the spring of her life at a winter wedding, Dad was 36.

My father was Patrick John Joseph McMenamin, an Irishman, born in Galway on the 10th June, 1919, his birthday one day before mine. He was the son of another Patrick, who had fought in the first world war and was a clerk at the labour exchange. My dad was the third of 11 children, two of his siblings died. In the early twentieth century Ireland was a poor country with a mostly rural population, life in Galway would have been hard for a big family. Dad fought against the odds, he persevered and studied hard through school. He was good at maths so when he finished his education, he went to work as a bookkeeper in a local module school, which was of such importance, it was used by University Hospital, Galway, to help with their research.

He was an intelligent, ambitious and good-looking young man and everyone said he looked a little like the American actor John Payne, with the addition of that easy, Irish charm. He was fit too, boxing regularly in local clubs, winning a trophy. The opportunities dwindled for a man like my father after the second world war, so, like many others before him, he came to England to seek his fortune. He got a job as a builder with Wimpey, constructing houses for the post-war generation and like every good immigrant, sent money back regularly to his family, as they were suffering from extreme poverty. Dad was named the family saviour for all his hard work and generosity. As soon as he was settled, he brought his brother's over to join him. Uncle Joe first as they were close in age and then Uncle Ray many years later as he was one of the youngest. It didn't take long before he progressed to a managerial level and travelled all over the UK, including to

Sawston, where he met my mum.

My parents brought me home from Dunstable hospital to our house on Half Moon Lane. A neat suburban street that ran off the High Street down to The Paddocks and Blow's Down Nature Reserve. Those were happy years. My earliest memories are the fleeting imprints left in a child's mind that develop into lasting memory. We went to my mother's parents a lot, my grandad and Nanny, and visited friends that were close enough for us children to call Aunty and Uncle – Verity and John. Their bungalow looked out over The Downs. I remember snowy days playing with my brothers, sledging down the glittering hillsides of Dunstable Downs. The cold biting through my mittens and the whipcrack wind rosying up my cheeks, my sharp fringe plastered to my head under a bobble hat, layered up in a hand-knitted cardigan glowing and refreshed after these family winter walks. Our family photographs show me as a smiling, golden-haired child, sandwiched between two cheeky brothers.

Dad was Catholic, my mother was not, but she was very happy for us to be brought up in the Catholic faith. On Sundays, Dad would take my brothers and I to church where I could sit on his lap instead of the hard pew, snuggled to his chest, keeping warm during the long service and enjoying a little exclusive father-daughter time. On the way home, we piled into the back of our Ford Anglia and he drove wibbly wobbly across the road. The three of us burst into excited bubbles of laughter, wide-eyed at the sudden swerves the car took. We never really felt we were in danger, we were safe with our dad.

On one occasion my father took me to his place of work. I must have only been about four years old and I was overawed by his smart office and large desk strewn with draftsmen's drawings. Maybe there were other implements of the building trade there too: hard hats, measuring equipment, telephones, technical drawings and men. It was an environment peopled almost solely by men in the 1960's. I do not recall being overawed by them, in later life I would find myself working in a male dominated environment, comfortable in their company. Maybe I was impressed with the importance of my father's role and by the assortment of practical things, but it sparked a lifelong interest in how things are made, how things work. I was never the little girl that demanded a doll, I was more interested in my older brother's Lego and Meccano, the '150 parts for all action fun.' I loved sketching and colouring too.

My love of drawing was encouraged on every visit to my grandparents. I was sat at the kitchen table and given large sheets of coloured sugar paper, "Helen, you're so good at drawing, do us a pattern like you usually do." My grandfather said, while he retired to the lounge in front of a great big fire and talked in hushed tones with my mother, father and nanny. I drew on the sugar paper to the background hum of their low voices. I knew something was wrong, but I wasn't quite sure what it was. Suddenly one day, all our belongings were in a new house. We had moved to be closer to my grandparents.

My father's illness was becoming a strain on my mother and we needed their support.

We moved in to number 19, The Limes, Sawston, just around the corner from nanny and grandad on Hillside. Dad had to give up work and Mum effectively became his nurse. Nobody told me about his illness, but with that intuition children have when adults talk in disguised whispers around them, I sensed something wasn't right. Dad became so ill, he was in bed all time. He was too poorly to join us on a trip to the coast at Sheringham with my grandparents, he wasn't there to jump the waves with me or build sandcastles on the beach. The happy days shrunk and soon we had to be quiet in the house. My father changed from a physical, vibrant man into an invalid. He had bowel cancer and as it ravaged him, I got that vague, tight unsettling deep inside, like you get when your parents are not there, and you're not sure when they will come back.

It wasn't until one day in August 1967 that I realised how wrong things were. I was sitting on the kerb outside our semi, the concrete warm through my thin dress, watching ants breaking through cracks in the pavement edge and chucking tiny stones into the road with another girl from the street, when out of the blue I asked, "Why is my family not here?"

"They've gone to your dad's funeral." She replied.

"What's a funeral?" I asked. I was five.

When my family finally returned, I followed them into the house, where I found my brothers and my mother, sat quietly on the Draylon sofa in the living room. The air was still and heavy with sorrow, thick in the August heat, everyone was sobbing. Someone said to me, I don't remember who, "Daddy's died."

I pretended to cry like the others, to be sad, but I didn't know what it meant, any of it. I can't remember if they told me he passed away before they had the funeral. My memory is of that hot day 1st August 1967, and our darkened living room. Life changed significantly after that.

5

BRICKS AND MORTAR

I was just five years old when my father died, he was only 48. My brother Paul was ten years old, David eight, my mother, 32. We were a young family suddenly alone without a paternal influence. Mum went back to work sometime after the funeral, at the Simplex Factory telephone exchange where she operated the switchboard on reception. For a few months I was left in the care of a cleaning lady, Mrs Hammond. She would take me with her to her jobs around Sawston and I'd watch her carry out her domestic duties, learning skills I could use to help our family. This continued for a few months until I started school. I went to the John Faulkner primary school nearby in Mill Lane. Mum took me on the first day, in my little green gingham school dress. I was terrified and not long after she left, I wet myself and had to be given something else to wear. So, like many children, my first experience of school was tinged with the memory of wearing something that did not fit that was out of the lost property box. It wasn't an uncommon first experience for a child starting school and I settled down after about two weeks and started to enjoy it. By the age of five I was walking myself to school. It was about a quarter of a mile, but I did not have to cross a road until I came to the lollipop lady at the bottom of the High Street.

For the first year my brothers would be at home with me after school but after a year I was usually on my own, David would be out playing football with his friends and Paul had started secondary school in Cambridge, so he got home much later. While I waited for Mum to come home I devised a domestic routine of my own. I cleaned the grate and re-set the fire, to be lit when she got in. Made sure the tools for the hearth were tidy. I loved to play with the shiny, brass coal scuttle, miniature dustpan and brush. Then I'd do the washing up and hoover the budgie seeds off the floor below Joey's cage, I didn't want to give my mum any excuse to get rid of him, I loved having a pet to look after.

They were straightened times after my father's death. Our house was not lavish, we had a small front room, a small dining room and a tiny kitchen. There was a wooden lean to, which my brother's and I commandeered as our playroom, built on the back of the house. The kitchen had a small worksurface, electric cooker and a pantry. It wasn't big enough for a family to eat in, we had a table in the dining room which we sat at for meals. Mother was no Cordon Bleu cook, but I expect she made the best of what we had, still, meals were basic and thin, meat and two veg, Vesta curries from the packet that only needed boiling water adding, baked beans on toast with Angel Delight and jelly for afters if we were lucky, and if we were really lucky we had ice cream.

I spent a lot of time on my own when I was little, I had a lot of freedom. These days it might be classed as neglect. There was no one to look after us and little food, especially at lunchtime when there were no free school meals. At first, we went to the factory canteen, but this was probably quite expensive for Mum, so soon ceased. At the time, I was very lonely but understood that Mum had to work, now I see our mother could have done more for us. My grandparents, who lived nearby and were not hard up, could have intervened more, but I at that time had little understanding about appropriate family care. We did visit them regularly. Sometimes I would call in on my way home after school. Their house was huge compared to ours and with the perspective of a child, with a large kitchen and lounge that was furnished with chairs lined up like a cinema row in front of the TV and the open fire. I'd sit in there and try to chat with my Nanny whilst Grandad popped in and out glancing at the racing or the snooker which was always on the TV. Nanny did not seem very interested in my company.

She treated the front parlour as a storage room, piling it high with boxes and books. On the occasions that my mum came with us, she squeezed between the flotsam and jetsam of my grandparent's storage space to the piano in the corner, lifted the lid and played a tune. Mum had learned to play the piano at school. I didn't inherit her musical ability, when I auditioned for the school choir, I was so bad the teacher thought I was deliberately mucking about and gave me a detention.

My grandparents helped sometimes, they took us to the dentist when my mother was working and on a few trips to the seaside on the Norfolk coast. We piled into grandad's big car where I was sandwiched on the bench seat in the front between him and nanny, Mum sat in between my brothers in the back. On the way there we'd stop at a pub close to the coast for a drink. Us children were treated to a coke and packet of crisps whilst the adults enjoyed a cold lager. When we got to the beach we were allowed an ice cream, a real treat! On the way home, we stopped at a hotel for dinner, an extravagant day out which ended with me perched at the table, sitting on my hands, envious and forlorn as my brothers tucked into huge knickerbocker glories, dipping long handled spoons into layers of cold, white ice cream, tinned fruit salad and glistening chocolate sauce, topped with a cherry nestling in a bed of whipped cream. I stared as they devoured their portions, clinking their spoons to the bottom of the empty sundae glass. I hadn't finished my dinner, a punishable sin for the adults of a war generation, used to rations and living without, a plate had to be clear before you could get any afters or treats. I never got any knickerbocker glory.

Being left alone so much taught me independence at home and gave me the opportunity to get away with things behind my mother's back, like the secret hamster. Mum worked all the time, she cycled to work for nine in the morning at the Simplex machine factory where they made machinery for the dairy industry. I longed for a pet to keep me company, and thought a hamster wouldn't be too much trouble, but my mother said no. David encouraged me to get one anyway. We bought a hamster from some local people and made sure they delivered the hamster at 4.30 p.m., knowing full well our mother would still be at work. When they arrived, we made excuses for her absence, "Mum's running late, she's been delayed at work, but she says it's fine for us to have the hamster." We fibbed. The truth was she knew nothing about it. I called our secret hamster Hammy. David and I put him in his cage and stored him under the bed in my bedroom. I had the box room, my brothers shared one of the other two bedrooms.

Housework was not one of our Mums' favourite pastimes, so even though she probably could not afford it, we had a lady who used to come in and help with the cleaning. Her name was Mrs Christian and she did two hours a week. One day Mum told us, "Mrs Christian's going to hoover under the beds today, make sure it's tidy." Given the advance notice, we put Hammy in the shed. We did this on all the days Mrs Christian came. Hammy did not remain a secret at Junior school, I told everyone about my new pet until the teacher said I could bring him in to show the class. I carefully carried him down the back path, a very quiet footpath that led to School. When I reached the street, I realised Hammy wasn't in his cage. I spent hours retracing my route back to the house and searched for him in every room. Eventually I turned up at school, late, sobbing and inconsolable. I never did find Hammy. I just hope he survived and went feral in Sawston village.

I started John Paxton Junior school in 1969. I walked myself to school again, fortunately it wasn't as far. We could wear what we wanted to at John Paxton, yet, as we had very few clothes, Mum insisted we should wear the school uniform, a white shirt, green skirt and green jumper in my case. I am sure most of my clothes came from jumble sales and my jumpers frequently had holes in them. One lunchtime, a teacher asked me to hand my jumper over to her and when she gave it back to me, the holes had disappeared, she had darned them all. I was so happy that I had to show my mum as soon as she got home. There were about 200 pupils at the school and only ten wore uniform, so I did feel different at school, somehow apart from everyone else, even though I had friends and was happy. I was lucky to have two especially good teachers. Mrs Phillips for the first two years and Mrs Chivers for the last two. They made such an impact on their young pupils. Mrs Philips would play her guitar in the shade of trees on the playing fields on sunny days, I loved singing along with the words from our little music books.

There was an outdoor swimming pool at the school which the children could use in the summer holidays, only if they were accompanied by their parents. My parent was working and couldn't accompany us, we couldn't tag on to another family, so my brother and his friend Trevor and I climbed over the fence at the back and swam when it was not being used. Until we were discovered. When the new term started my brother David and Trevor were hauled up in assembly and given a good telling off in front of the whole school. I escaped this punishment as I was off school with chicken pox, but I was still called in to see the headmaster when I returned, for a severe dressing down.

I did well in school. My reading ability was well beyond my age, so I was often used as a good example and asked to read aloud in class. Reading was the one thing I could do on my own, it was my escape into another world. I would spend hours in the local library in the company of adventure stories and non-fiction books and at Christmas, when books were given as gifts, I loved to tear open the wrapping on editions of *The Famous Five* and *The Secret Seven*. These tales of independent, adventurous children who solved mysteries without the help of any grownups resonated with me. I was learning to make my own adventures.

I loved riding my bicycle. One day, grandad turned up with a new bike, well, it was new to me. It was so big he had got someone to screw wooden blocks to the pedals which meant I could just about ride it. I still had my little bike when I was eight years old and Paul got me to cycle all the way from Sawston to Cambridge with him, about 12 miles, so he could go and look at some new stamps in Heffers, the nearest book and stamp emporium. When Mum found we were missing, she asked a car-owning friend if they could drive out and look for us. They discovered us in Trumpington, on our way home. They put my bike in the back of the car and took me home. Paul was made to finish the journey alone. He got into so much trouble for taking me with him, but I escaped a telling off.

My eldest brother Paul was a clever young man who was into chemistry. He carried out home-grown experiments in the playroom at the back of our house. One such experiment went a little bit wrong when he blew the top off the twin tub washing machine. He had his chemistry set taken away then, so he transferred his interest to electronics. Someone had given us an old black and white portable television that we kept up in our bedroom. I loved watching TV up there, especially in the school holidays when morning programmes were *The Adventures of Heidi* or *White Horses*. It was a different matter when we wanted to watch TV after bedtime. Mum was always telling us to turn it off, marching up the stairs and catching us in the act, so Paul rigged an electronic alarm under the carpet on the bottom stair, which triggered if someone stood on it. It gave us enough of a warning to turn off the TV set and dive into bed, snuggling under the covers and pretending we were asleep, the very picture of innocence, before Mum opened the bedroom door.

Mum loved a gin and tonic of an evening and she wasn't easy to wake up. When she fell asleep, my brother David and I climbed out of our bedroom window along the lean-to, keeping tight into the wall of the house so we didn't put our feet through the roof, we climbed over the garage and down an oil tank at the end. We called for our friend, Trevor, who lived in a bungalow at the end of our cul-de-sac. Then we then went to the end of our garden, climbed over the fence and followed the back path until we reached our friend Sally Cook's house. She was supposed to be waiting for us but was not. Trevor and my brother thought it would be a good idea to throw tiny stones at her bedroom window to wake her up. Unfortunately, Sally's dad heard us, opened the window and shouted at us to go home. Our gang was down from the "Famous Four" to the intrepid three, but we kept on our adventure. We dare not walk down the main roads in case we were spotted so we travelled down the tiny back paths, coming to the long drive that led up to the Tudor manor house. It was supposed to be haunted by ghosts like Mary Queen of Scots who hid there on the way to claim the throne in 1553 and was later executed. This information put the frights up me. My heart was pounding, palms slicked with sweat and I gripped my brother's hand and we proceeded up the long drive under the dark oaks and rustling ash trees. I was sure I could hear the whisper of ghosts echoing through the velvety night. I only made it half way down the dark drive before I panicked and snatched my hand from my brothers. I turned tail and ran home as fast as I could, the boys followed me. I grew braver in daylight when we sneaked into Sawston hall again, clambering into the boat that was moored in the moat and rowing it through the murky water. We were discovered once and chased out of the grounds.

Then when I was about seven, Mum brought another person into our family. She fostered a young girl Pat, who was about 17 and obviously not happy at home. Mum was grateful for the extra money the foster caring brought in, and she and Mum became very good friends. I gave up my bedroom and moved back in with my brothers, they had a bunk bed and I was given a small single opposite them. Pat was a nice girl and I didn't feel any jealousy or animosity towards her, she lived with us for some time, married young and I was her bridesmaid.

When I was about ten years old, all three siblings were still living at home, but our family did not stay together much longer. My oldest brother, Paul, was always the bossy one, perhaps he saw himself as the man of the house after the death of my father, either way, he wanted to be in control, to be in charge. To his younger siblings he was the boss, but we eventually grew tired of his dictatorial ways. It got too much for us one day when David and I locked him out of the house. We ran up to the third step on our stairs, so we could reach the telephone, meaning to call Mum and tell on him. Paul tried to put a stop to our plans, as we struggled with the dial on the phone he approached the long window above the stairs and in his anger and frustration, smashed straight through it, shattering glass over David and me. From that moment on, he went to live with my grandparents around the corner, he

54

always had a close relationship with our grandfather and I was envious that he was given his own room and a record player.

I'd come to love music too, at the beginning of secondary school my favourites were The Bay City Rollers and The Monkees. I had the cut off tartan trousers, and the scarf, that marked myself as a true 'rollers' fan, I loved glam rock and The Sweet too. I was one of the youngest in my class and I took my 11 plus in the hope that I could go to St. Mary's convent in Cambridge, but I failed. There was no way I was going to the village college in Sawston, I wanted to go to St. Bede's in Cambridge, where my brother's went. Our father had been a Catholic, and although our mother wasn't, she did want us to keep his faith and sent us to Sunday school and a Catholic school, St. Bedes in Cherry Hinton, just outside Cambridge. The headteacher there was Mr Kent, he was such a wonderful man who played a fatherly role in our family. From the moment I met him I felt comfortable in his presence and loved listening to him in assembly. Later on in life he wrote me a lovely letter saying how proud he was of me.

My relationship with my mother was something of a roller coaster when I was growing up. She was not around as much as I would have liked, but I loved her to bits. As I grew older she became more like a friend than a mother, sometimes our roles reversed, and I felt more like the adult in the relationship. She didn't spend much time with us when we were young, not at weekends when she would go to Lakenheath air base and leave us on our own, a nine-year-old, a seven-year-old and five-year-old me. She'd leave in a cloud of hair spray and perfume and come back much later with men from the base, smelling of stale cigarettes and alcohol. The record player would be brought out and the drinking would continue while I lay awake upstairs listening to the party. Mum had a lot of boyfriends, some short-term, some lasted longer. There were a few that were nice and one lovely one, unfortunately he was already married. He took us for day trips on his boat on the Great Ouse river in Ely. One of Mum's boyfriends took us to the local fair, but he spent all the money my mother had given him for her children's entertainment on the slot machines.

Mum seemed to be attracted to some men who were no good. Basil Kitchen was one of her first boyfriends, a weaselly looking, ginger-haired bloke she met in Sawston. He came to the house when the four of us were home and I was about six years old, "Let's go for a drive Helen." He suggested. I had no reason to think he might be up to no good, so I agreed. He drove us out to a pub in Whittlesford village and told me to stay in the car while he went to the bar and bought a drink. He came out with a packet of crisps for me and dangled them tantalizingly over my head, "You can have these Helen, if you get in there." He said, pointing to the boot of his car. I climbed in, crisps were a rare treat and I was hungry. He shut the boot and left me there for half an hour or so while he went back into the pub to finish his drink. Heavens knows what he had in mind, or whether he did it in spite to punish my Mum, either way, he must have changed his mind and he took me home.

I had a lucky escape. Mum finished with him soon after, perhaps she found out what he had done, although I never told her. Basil didn't accept Mum had finished with him, he came to the house afterwards and smashed it to bits. We had to all go and spend the night in a nearby hotel as it was too dangerous to return until the police found and arrested him.

My mother had one particular friend called Lillian, a lady with shiny blonde hair and a wide smile, who was married, but separated with a couple of kids. Mum took to going up to the air force base with her on nights out. Lillian sold clothes door-to-door. There were a lot of door-to-door sales in the late 60's and early 70's. There was Avon, the pop man with his clinking van of Corona bottles of lime green, cola and strawberry, a milkman, the rag and bone man for rubbish and useless objects, an egg van and a bread van. Lillian owned a van too, a minivan, it was just like the minicar, but with double doors and a van base at the back. She drove us to Weston Super Mare near Bristol, 189 miles along the A1 and the M4, four of us in the back of this little van, her son John, myself and my brother's, rattling around like pop bottles about to explode in the heat. I think we must have stayed in a sort of Bed and Breakfast. We had the downstairs rooms and the owner had the upstairs, with a door over the top of the stairs. Us children were alone in our part of the house at night, whilst my mum and Lillian went out. One night the boys made me watch a Dracula film on TV. I was terrified and crying so much that the woman who owned the Bed and Breakfast heard and came downstairs.

When she found us alone she took me upstairs until Mum got back, then told my mother off for leaving us on our own. It didn't seem to deter Mum, there were plenty of other occasions when she left us to our own devices.

There were other occasions when we had better holidays with Mum. In 1971, a year I will never forget, we hired a caravan on the Norfolk coast at Hunstanton. I was nine years old. It was just our little family, my Mum, brothers and me. The caravan opposite owned a dog called Piola that was often tethered outside. I spent every day making a big fuss of that dog, we loved each other's company. If we went to the beach, I abandoned the search for fossils or digging sandcastles and I was reluctant to paddle in the sea. I had to get back and see Pialo. When we got home, Mum arranged a very special birthday present for me, a little Yorkshire terrier that cost 45 guineas, that was a lot of money then as we still did not have much. The day he arrived I refused to go to my friend's birthday party as there was no way I could leave him. His pedigree name was Mulbarton Fred, so I decided to call him Fred. Maybe Mum sympathised, maybe it was guilt, but I was eternally grateful that she noticed my feelings about Piola in Norfolk and responded by getting me a dog of my own.

Fred became my constant playmate and companion. As soon as I picked up my book he would be by my side. I was convinced he was reading it with me. He always protected me when I was having arguments with my brothers and I sometimes took him for walks in my doll's pram. He slept on my bed at night, until my mum got a new husband, who soon put a stop to that.

Before my Great Aunty Alice passed away, she came to live in Sawston in sheltered accommodation and I'd visit her every Saturday afternoon. I'd make a pot of tea and bring out the special biscuits she bought for us, Jaffa Cakes with their thick, dark chocolate and sweet orange marmalade. We would watch the wrestling together, Mick McManus and Giant Haystacks. We loved each other's company and laughed a lot together. I would give her a big hug when I left, and she insisted on giving me 50p, a lot of money in those days.

I became closer to my mother's brother, Uncle John. Granddad used his influence as a Freemason and helped my Uncle John buy a newsagent's business in Sawston. Mandevilles was a large shop that was very popular in the village. Uncle John sometimes asked me to cover for paperboys and do an evening round if someone was ill. I couldn't have a regular round as I was still living in Sawston and catching two buses to get home from School so did not get home until about 5 p.m. When I was older, Uncle John asked if I would like to work in the shop during the holidays, which was great, even thought I had to travel by bus from Cambridge. Suddenly I had lots of pocket money. Uncle John always looked out for me, there was a closeness and warmth in our relationship which was missing with other, older male family members. He lived about ten-minute walk away from my grandparents in Sawston and I'd see him at my grandparents on family get togethers.

Sometimes he would come around and play cards with us at The Limes on a Sunday night. John married a lovely lady called Rosemary, who had a daughter, Amanda, three or four years younger than me. I stayed with Amanda one night as John and Rosemary were going out and we became close friends. I always enjoyed their company and loved going over as it was such a warm and relaxing family environment.

My Mum and Dad on their wedding day, early 1956, January

Paul on the left, Mum, Valerie crouched in centre with me on her knee and David on the right, summer 1962

Indoor version of previous photograph, this time they gave me a music box to keep me still – Paul on left, me on Mum's knee, Mum in a snazzy pair of glasses and David on the right. I'm about two years old

Three in a row with my brothers

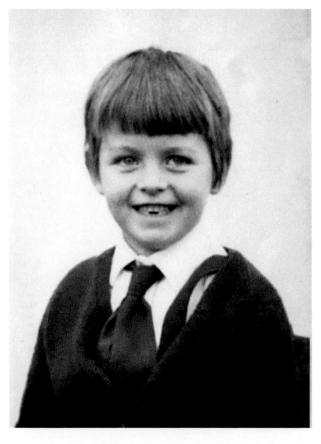

Shortly after starting school

On the beach with Mum and Dad

Maisie's daughter's wedding – around 1966

Me and my bike

6

SYSTEM CHANGES

It may have been my grandad who created an introduction to Jack. They were both freemasons at the Cambridge Masonic Lodge in Bateman Street. The lodge was a powerful organisation that had been in existence since 1836. It was a men's club with charitable responsibilities and a mission to look after family. My grandfather might have thought a fellow Mason holding the responsible position of Chief Inspector in the Cambridge police force, would be a stable influence and a good match for his daughter. Things didn't quite work out as he had planned.

Jack began visiting my mum. Their relationship blossomed, and they decided to buy a house together in Cambridge, 107 Perse Way, not far from the Cambridge City Football ground. It was a neat, 1960's semi with a fenced garden, on a road with wide grass verges and oak trees, a small step up from The Limes and no longer around the corner from my grandparents. Jack had been married before and had one son, Keith, who was at Keele University and therefore not able to visit very often. The new house had three bedrooms, one large and two medium size. David and I were to share the large bedroom and one of the rooms was to be saved for Keith. Mum and Jack were married in 1976 at the Shire Hall registry office in Cambridge and held the reception back at our new house.

From the start, my brother David didn't get on with Jack, he went from being the man of the house at 14, to having a man telling him what to do all the time. A strict and influential man who quickly moved up the police ranks to the role of Superintendent. Their relationship strained the atmosphere in the house and agitated the fractures in our family. Mum and Jack's relationship was fractious from the start. They could both drink heavily at social occasions, when they went out, and weekends at home. It was drink that fuelled the emotional atmosphere. At times, it was like living in a tinder box at home, one spark, one argument, and the whole thing blew up. I was only 12 and didn't quite understand the complicated workings of the lives of grownups, but I was aware of the change in the system, the shift in atmosphere and the souring of the peace. I clung to familiar things to cope, to my friends, my school and my dog, Fred.

Jack had imposed a ban on Fred sleeping on my bed throughout the night. Fred cried so much when he was left him on his own, and I couldn't bear it. I snuck downstairs to the kitchen, put a blanket on the floor next to Fred's basket, and laid beside him until he was asleep, then I tiptoed back to my room. As soon as my stepfather came down to the kitchen, in the morning and opened the door, Fred dashed upstairs and onto my bed. David and I subverted Jack's rule in other ways. He had packed his son, Keith's, Scalextric track away in a cupboard, we were told not to play with it, but we longed to, and as soon as Jack went to work, we got the Scalextric out of the cupboard, clicked the pieces together across the living room floor and connected up our cars, racing them wildly around the track until they flew off at speed and hit the walls. We made sure there were no marks or evidence of our use, tidying up the crime scene to leave no evidence and tucked the Scalextric back in the cupboard before Jack came home.

It wasn't long before there were more upheavals in the structure of our family. My nanny passed away in 1976, the same year my mum was remarried. I was old enough to go to my nanny's funeral and was very sad. On reflection, she gave me little time and attention, unlike her lovely sister, Great Aunty Alice. Shortly after, an old family friend returned from Canada where she had been living near her daughter. Maisie was a widow herself, she had one daughter and a son who was gay, openly so, which was a rarity in the early 70's. Maisie was a fancy lady and very keen on keeping up appearances. It wasn't long before she took up with my grandad and moved in with him to the house in Sawston. She set about making changes, turning the front room that my nanny had used as a storeroom into a palatial living room, with fancy furniture and new carpets and redecorating to her taste. She installed French doors from the living room which led to a new conservatory that opened out onto the large lawn. Granddad often opened a bottle of champagne there, he liked his fizz.

My brother Paul was still living with them then, he didn't seem to object to Maisie's presence and it didn't seem to matter to my mother that her father was living with another woman. She knew Maisie from before she had moved to Canada. Before my father died, my mother was happy for me to be bridesmaid at Maisie's daughter's wedding. I was about four years old and it was a rare occasion for me to be squashed into a dress, a full-length smock at that, with a bonnet. I looked like Little Bo Peep who had lost her sheep, swinging a spherical bouquet from a long ribbon like a weapon. The wedding was at St. Mary's church in Sawston and the reception was in the lovely grounds of Sawston Hall, grounds I explored with my brother, David, at all times of the day and night when I was older.

Other family members were not so accepting of Maisie. My Great Aunty Alice, my nanny's sister who I was very close to, was very upset when I told her. We were enjoying our usual cup of tea on a Saturday afternoon and I said that I had recently met Maisie around Grandads. I saw immediately that she was extremely upset, and I believe that grandad perhaps had had a bit of a fling with her in the past. Alice and grandad then had a big falling out and sadly, Alice died a couple of months later before there was any reconciliation. I was heartbroken.

At age 12 I had started at St. Bede's Roman Catholic secondary school in Cambridge, finally able to be at the same school my brothers attended. It was a wonderful place and formed a very important part of my life. Everybody wore a school uniform and, as we were now better off, I had a decent one. The headmaster was Mr Kent who I called the gentle giant because he was so tall, but good and kind to me. Then there was Mr Ball the deputy head. He was also wonderful and did so much for everyone. I remember him taking us to one of our netball matches one Saturday and as we were driving back he said, "Would you like to stop off at that fair over there girls?" We were delighted to go to the fair. There was so much to do outside of school - netball matches, hockey matches and my favourite sport, tennis. We also did sponsored walks, sponsored fasting and the Duke of Edinburgh awards. Suddenly my life had changed for the better, becoming richer and fuller. In terms of study my favourite subjects were English literature and English language and my poetry was often read in class. I was a determined pupil and had some wonderful teachers like Mr Fraser who taught me physics. He was an inspirational man who pushed me in the direction of the career I pursued. In terms of science studies in my last two years at school, I had the choice of doing biology or chemistry and physics or domestic science. I chose biology and physics. I loved school and had some wonderful friends and to boost my confidence I was the first girl in our year to be asked out by a very good-looking boy, David Quinn. We stayed together for at least two years.

After we had moved to Cambridge and I was in my second

year at St. Bedes, my family was fragmenting and changing. The tension at home bubbled upwards like mercury in a thermometer. Boiling arguments between my mum and my stepfather were followed by periods of icy silence around the dinner table. The atmosphere was unhappy and stifling, so I began to search elsewhere for other groupings that would nurture and support me in place of the family that was lacking at home.

Shortly after we moved to Perse Way, I met the family that lived diagonally opposite and made friends with their daughter, Jane Trippet, who also went to St. Bedes School. She and her parents, Jim and Ena, took me to church with them, they became like a surrogate family to me, my rock in a difficult childhood. Jane had five wonderful siblings. Jill, Steve, Peter, Pat and Mick, who also, always made me feel welcome. There was only Jane and Jill still living at home at that time but on Christmas Eve we all went to midnight mass and then went back to Jane's house to open presents. I got home after Mum and Jack. There were many lovely Italians at St. Bede's and a lot of them became very good friends. Jane married one of them, Nino, and me and Jill were bridesmaids at their wedding. Jane and I remain firm friends.

During our formative years we spent a lot of time together, going to school discos and dancing, walking our dogs Fred and Sandy and going away on holidays together. In the long, hot summer of 1976, we went to stay with Jane's Aunty Fanny, a retired headteacher who lived in Blackpool. We spent most of our time on the beach, or at Pleasureland, we saved up all our pocket money and spent it on hot doughnuts, fairground rides and the penny machines. Aunty Fanny fed us and sometimes took us out for lunch in the pubs and cafés along the front. It was with Jane and her family that I went on my first holiday abroad, aged 17, to Spain. We loved the apartment, the sun and the beach and the numbers of nice young men at the local disco. Jane's dad had to come and pick us up and keep an eye on us.

I was also friends with Neil, who lived across the road at Perse Way. He lived with his mum and his sister, Vanda. When their mum went out, Neil, his friend Mark and I would buy a bottle of Strongbow cider to share at their house while we listened to music. I had the first Dire Straits LP on vinyl and was partial to a bit of 'Saturday Night Fever' by the Bee Gees too. Neil's dad was a taxi driver and took us to Cromer on the coast for the day. Neil's dad was able to use the social club at Cambridgeshire County Council's offices in Shire Hall Club, as taxi drivers were employed by the council, and he let us go with him and his brother's. Neil, Mark and I learned to play snooker there. I became proficient, and like Paul Newman in *The Hustler*, would delight in taking the older and more experienced players down.

Between friends, their families, school and sports, I was getting by, surviving the background of my fractured family, but then there was another trauma lying in wait, another adversity looming that I would need to overcome. In the long, hot summer of 1976 I was 14, settled at school and doing well. My brother David was 16 and had left school. It may have been tempers and irritations were strained in the long drought and the stifling heat, but David found himself in a situation in Cambridge city centre, which quickly escalated into a physical dispute. He was involved in a fight with other friends and was arrested. It went to court. Much to our shock, my brother and his friend Robert were sentenced to six months in a youth detention centre, North Sea Camp, on the coast. My stepfather could have intervened, given his position as a policeman and a Freemason, he would have had some influence, but it may be that he used this influence with the judge, and had something to do with the harsh sentence they received. Perhaps he wanted to get David out of the way or to teach him a lesson. Either way, it had a huge impact on my brother's life, he was never the same afterwards. I felt terrible about it. Mr Kent, the headmaster at St. Bedes was supportive, he behaved as a father figure to me, he was distressed that this had happened to two ex-pupils. Mum was very upset. It couldn't have helped her relationship with Jack. We visited David by train or got a lift with a friend, Jack never took us, and I wrote to my brother all the time in an effort to keep his spirits up.

By the time I was 14 I was left as the only sibling living at home with Mum and Jack. I got on all right with Jack, but I was never completely at ease in his company. He was a man more reserved than tactile and I never thought of him as a father. He made some efforts to protect me in his own way.

When I was older and working I was out for dinner with them in Cambridge and waiting at the bus stop for the bus home, when one of the blokes from the design department came rushing across the road to give me a hug, Jack thought he was about to attack me and nearly smacked him one.

It wasn't long into Mum and Jack's marriage that the arguments started. I was stranded in the middle of their sniping and bickering. They both drank too much. Jack would have a few drinks when they went out for meals and drive home, he was never stopped or arrested for drink driving, his masonic connections ensured he got away with it. On Saturday mornings I was paid 50p to clean the whole house. Tidy, hoover and dust as well as cleaning the bathroom and downstairs toilet. Mum drank nearly a bottle of sherry at lunchtime and fell asleep in the afternoon, then she'd go out in the evening for more drinks. She was working at Taylor Vintners solicitors at the time. At dinnertime the three of us sat around the table. I stared at my plate wishing the ground would swallow me up as they argued or sat in icy silence. The tension distressed me so much that I developed an eating disorder. When faced with a special or formal, sit down meal, I just couldn't eat, I was trapped by the anxiety my mum and Jack had created around these occasions. As my career blossomed I had to seek some specialist help via my GP.

At night I'd lie in my bed in and listen to them argue, tensing my body with stress. A lot of the arguments were my Mum's fault. If they went out together, she would drink too much and start to flirt with other men, taunting Jack. He hated this. Maybe her behaviour was a way of railing against his rule, she didn't want her wings clipped. By then I had started a new chapter in life which gave me a focus away from my difficult home life, a focus that directed my ambition and fulfilled the desire to move away from home, discovering and befriending colleagues who supported and nurtured me better than my own family could. I had started work.

7

WELDED TO LIFE

By the time I was 15 I was studying hard and had taken two of my 'O' levels early. I would rather be at my desk in my bedroom at home than downstairs with Jack and my mother. Despite being a capable student, I said no to 'A' levels, I wanted to get away from the toxic atmosphere in the house as soon as possible, further study would have meant staying at home and I had the idea to get a job, rent a room and move out. At St. Bede's I had supportive and influential teachers who make such a difference to a young person's life, like my physics teacher, Mr Fraser. I chose to do physics instead of cookery. Mr Fraser asked me, "What do you want to be when you leave school Helen?" and I answered, "I don't know, but I don't want to be a nurse or a secretary." There was no way I was going to conform to the stereotypical career options given to girls in the late 1970's. Mr Fraser recognised there were other options open to me, he built up my confidence. When I was 15 and in my last year of school, he encouraged me to go to an open day at the Welding Institute in Abingdon.

The Welding Institute was the professional membership arm of the internationally renowned engineering research and technology organisation TWI. By the late 1970's it was at the forefront of research into welding, joining and associated technologies, producing academic documents, guidelines for industry and recommendations to government. It was a very significant place, imposing too, based in the grounds of a former eighteenth century manor house, where it had moved in 1946, with a tree lined drive and swathes of woodland either side.

I went there with Paul Evans from school, six foot six to my five foot three, we must have made a mismatched pair. When we arrived, they gave us a coffee and told us all about what the institute did and who their customers were. There were about 60 people in total and I noticed I was one of the few girls. Then they broke us up into smaller groups and showed us around all the different departments. I was so impressed and interested. When we returned we were given a bit of lunch and then given a test. A few days later I was told by my teacher Mr Fraser that they had selected 12 from the day to go forward to interview. I was one of them. Paul was chosen too.

On the day of the interview I had to get the bus to Abington and walk to the Welding Institute which was probably half a mile. It was snowing heavily, which made it a difficult and cold walk, not helped by the fact I was wearing my school uniform and my trendy blue clogs. On arrival I was perched in front of a panel of six men. I felt overwhelmed, diminished and more than a little nervous as the interview began. I began to relax when they asked me what books I liked to read. I'd always read widely and loved books, I'd recently finished Dickens, *Great Expectations*, which we had studied at school, and began to discuss it with passion. Perhaps they approved of my own expectation and ambition, but out of the six apprenticeships they offered that year, two went to myself and Paul. I started in the July, soon after I turned 16.

My grandfather must have been proud of my achievement as he bought me a 50cc moped for my birthday, and Mum bought me the helmet. It was quite a journey to work, about 12 miles each way in all weathers, and my bike was not very powerful. It had a problem with the engine and I struggled up Huckeridge Hill, the only hill for miles around, revving the gears as I almost tilted into a wheelie. On days when the weather was too bad to use my bike, where icy roads meant I would be slip sliding along, someone from work gave me a lift. Lift sharing was quite a common practice, and I always paid my way for fuel. Some of the people I worked with were generous and kind, nurturing a young apprentice and becoming good friends over the years.

My first six weeks were spent in the machine shop where I was taken under the wing of the person in charge of training, Colin Hardy. He was one of several work colleagues who became a major influence on me, a very important person in my career and personal life. I hadn't done any metalwork at school, but I was soon challenged with learning how to use all the equipment, despite my lack of experience. They gave me various tasks to develop my skills on the lathe, drilling machine and grinding machine, making a scribe which marks metal and a hole punch marker. Hardly stuff that would change the face of engineering, but it gave me a good grounding in the basics and the confidence to take on more.

The industrial size lathes and grinders orchestrated a cacophony of noise, of metal on metal, the machines whirring and drilling. The workshop smelled of hot metal, burning machines and plenty of testosterone. There were 20 men working in the machine shop and I was the only girl that had ever worked there. Come the tea break at 10 a.m., they would share their tea and biscuits with me and not hold their conversation in check in the presence of a female. I remained nonchalant, held my own. I had two brothers at home and was used to a male environment. In the workshop, the men were friendly, but kept their distance. I don't think they knew what to make of a young, female work colleague. It wasn't a politically correct time and a lot of them had Page Three calendars up on the walls with their monthly shots of topless women. I never commented on theses calendars, and occasionally there would be the odd comment to gauge my response. I remained calm and unruffled. After a while, when they had got used to my presence and seeing how hard I worked, dressed in my jeans and practical clothes like them, or our green overalls in the workshop, they respected me as an equal, realised a woman was not an object and took the calendars down.

After six weeks in the machine shop I was sent to the welding research block where I learned gas welding and manual metal arc. The practical training was going well, after which I was sent to a department, Stress Wave Emission, where I spent another year. We tested the acoustic emissions made by metals as they deformed, testing materials before they were used in large scale structures such as oil rigs. I was analysing the output coming from the computer, a responsible, administrative post. To an extent it was boring, repetitive work, so when Duncan Rhead let me look round his department, Ultra High Vacuum Diffusion Bonding, I was very pleased when he asked me if I would be interested in working there. My boss at the time, Peter Bartlett, wanted to keep me in his department for at least another three months so that I could finish a project off. After this I moved over, applying my physics knowledge to a new area of work.

Ian Bucklow oversaw Ultra High Vacuum Diffusion Bonding, he proved, like many others throughout my career, to be a good bloke to work for, alongside Keith Johnson who was Head of department for microjoining. Keith and Ian both lived near Perse Way, so if I was stuck for a lift to work one of them would help. Glynn Hall worked in the department next door and became a good friend. But it was Duncan who became the best mentor and friend. He would often play practical jokes on me, asking me to go over the stores and pick up,

"A metric adjustable spanner." Only when I got to the stores and saw Mr Woolfords face did I realise it was a joke. Duncan persisted with other requests, but my knowledge and confidence had grown, and I soon twigged. After some time I asked my mum to help me plot my revenge. I gave her some detailed technical information and a mock job description for a non-existent post she was to offer Duncan. Mum took it seriously and revised the information as if she were preparing for an important acting role. She rang Duncan up and pretended to offer him an interview for this role on a much bigger salary, he was flattered and impressed and agreed to be interviewed. I let him believe the offer for a while before I eventually told him the truth. Glyn and I laughed for days. We would affectionately wind each other up throughout our working relationship and as well as Duncan and his wife Patsy, becoming friends to me, he became good friends with Mum too.

My mother could always be relied upon to execute practical jokes, she was the bright spark on many social situations and loved humour and comedy. She was still working at the solicitors, Taylor Vintners, and took me to their company cricket matches where she ensured there was no female relegation to making the tea and sandwiches in the pavilion and encouraged me to play in the team, laughing and clapping wildly as I hit the ball for six. When she went to the pubs in Cambridge drinking with her friends, she would take me along. On many occasions she would behave as a better mother than a friend. I loved her despite her downsides and our relationship was strong.

By this time, I was 17 and a half and beginning to strike out on my own, making moves towards independence. I wasn't a feminine teenager, I probably wore trousers too much, but then I had been brought up with two brothers and wanted to do everything they did, skirts just got in the way. I loved Dire Straits and Queen and developed a lot of sporting interests which flourished when I started work. I was in several different hockey clubs and tried water-skiing, which I went to with Paul Evans, my school mate who had secured a job alongside me at the institute and had become a good friend. A lot of my associates at the Welding Institute played squash, including my close friends, Duncan and Glynn and I started to go with them, meeting at the Leys School squash courts on Tuesday evenings. There were up to 12 of us at any one time, I was one of only two females. I became proficient at squash and enjoyed going for the drinks afterwards in the club. When I was 18, Mum offered boarding to a girl who was working in the chemical industry. Claire was based in Cambridge for a while and associated with one of the colleges, where she was in the rowing club. On one day, they were short of a team member and she asked if I would go along and give it a try. That's how I ended up rowing for the City of Cambridge Women's Rowing Club, one of the oldest in the city. I became part of a team of four, plus the cox, and took part in the Cambridge Bumps. In this race we were set off at different times along the river Cam, as soon as your boat caught up and 'bumped' the boat in front, they were out. Winners got their blades. I enjoyed rowing with the club, there was a good social life with plenty of after training drinking in the boathouse on Midsummer Common too.

Life flourished away from home and there were holidays without Mum and Jack. When I was just 16 in the summer of 1978, I took the train and boat to Ireland with my good friend from school, Anna Cafferky. My Aunty Ann who I had never met before, picked us up from the boat and drove us to the bus station to travel to Anna's relatives in County Mayo. The bus only went so far, we had to make our own way for the rest of the journey, getting a lift from the local artificial insemination man, who drove us the rest of the way in his van, stopping at several farms to drop off samples to inseminate the cows along the way. We stayed about two miles outside the neat, Georgian town of Westport with Anna's aunty and uncle, and their four children. Westport was a pretty place, with attractive streets and a bridge over the river, but it was a totally different way of life out at her aunt's house. It was a rural area and the famous mountain of Coragh Patrick, known locally as 'The Reek,' loomed over the house, where they had no inside toilet or water supply. We'd run down the garden to go to the outside 'privy' and explored the nearby woods and fields with her cousins. Our dinners were plain potatoes and eggs, until the day Anna's uncle caught a salmon in the local river and we had that for tea. It was a new experience for two girls from the Cambridge area. We went to church in Westport on the Sunday with all the family, the women retired to a room for coffee and tea afterwards and all the men went in the pub. Anna and I joined the men in the pub, much to their surprise.

After a week, we caught the bus to Galway where I had

the intention to meet some of my father's family for the first time. We stayed in a hotel near my Aunty Angela's and Aunty Joan came up from Limerick to meet us and stayed on for a few days. Anna and I explored the area with Aunty Angela's son and his friend. I was so very happy to finally be spending some time with my Dad's family. We headed down to nearby Silverstrand beach for a few ciders, its coffee cake cliffs were very like those at Hunstanton, perhaps that reminded me of home and where I wanted to be as we wandered along the shore by the Atlantic Ocean. Anna felt differently, Ireland was home to her and she decided to stay on. I came back to England on my own. Anna remained in Ireland for the rest of her life.

My quest for a life of independence continued. As soon as I was 17 I had taken driving lessons and passed on the second go of my test. I bought my first car, a blue Morris 1100 with vinyl seats, no radio and a choke, for £200. The poor car was not very reliable and a bit of a rust bucket, but as I worked in welding, a couple of the welders worked on it to keep it together. It was not unlike my life at home at the time, Mum was not reliable, she and Jack were always arguing, and as they fell apart my work colleagues helped me rebuild my life and overcome the adversity at home. Eventually my Morris 1100 just died. I couldn't sell it, so I gave it to a local secondary school for their mechanics to use. Then I bought a snazzy Renault 12. It was like driving a luxury car after the Morris, it had a radio and gears that were light and workable. Duncan at work helped organise the purchase of my cars for many years and Colin helped maintain and service them. I loved learning how to mend my car and being a hobby mechanic. It was another distraction form the unrest at home.

I was still very unhappy there. The arguments had got worse. Work provided a welcome escape and I started socialising more with my colleagues, taking any opportunity to stay out of the house for as long as possible now that I had a car to get me away. I went to the Welding Institute Social Club in Abingdon where they asked me to help behind the bar some evenings. This supplemented my meagre salary and gave me another place to be other than home. I enjoyed it there, so much, I booked the club for my 18 birthday party there and paid for it myself, Mum and Jack didn't, and invited all my work colleagues, friends and their girlfriends. Life was changing, I was moving away from friendships with women, Jane had a boyfriend by then, so I didn't see much of her anyway and Anna had stayed in Ireland. I worked in a male dominated environment, and it became the norm for my closest friendships to develop with my male work colleagues.

I began to confide in them, especially Duncan. I discussed my search for a flat share with him regularly, complaining about the mess in all the flats I viewed, I was clean and tidy and particularly fussy about where I wanted to live. Duncan knew how unhappy I was at home, so he suggested I try and buy a flat of my own, instead of renting and sharing. A small studio flat should just be within my reach. He researched a company that would give me a mortgage of £17,000, with no deposit, which helped me to buy a flat in Amwell Road North Arbury, Cambridge. It was a studio flat with a little kitchen, a living area with a table for eating and a settee that turned into a bed at night. There was a tiny dressing area, a bathroom with a sink, toilet and shower. It was perfect, plenty big enough for me. At last I had my own space. I could sleep at night without the sound of vicious arguments leaking through the walls. Most of my salary went on the mortgage and food, but I was able to earn some extra money for weekend on call as Duncan had set up a research project that needed 24-hour monitoring.

By the time the new decade dawned I was 19, young, determined and finally living in my own place. I loved having that hard won and valuable independence, but life was about to throw another curve ball at me, I wouldn't be on my own for long.

8

FORGED IN FIRE

In the decade between 1980 and 1990 I forged ahead with my career. It was unusual for a woman to reach the positions I did within that era, especially in the field of engineering, but my career development did not seem particularly unique to me. It followed a natural progression as I loved researching my field and co-operating with, then leading, a team. At the beginning of the 80's, Duncan had me working on the 'hydrogen bomb' project, so called because the metal structures we were stress testing for oil platforms and the like contained hydrogen.

I went to the department where the research project was taking place three or four times a day and it was while I was there that I noticed a young guy in the workshop. He was handsome, with short, fair hair, well-spoken and educated and engaged me in conversation at every opportunity. Richard Davenport was taller, and older than me by about four years. He had a self-effacing charm that I found particularly attractive and would play down his academic contacts, referring to himself as just, 'a hairy-arsed welder.' His father had been a professor at Cambridge and he came from an academic family, although he would play down his academic contacts. He'd been expelled from school, or 'asked to leave' as the private school he went to would have it. Like me, he had lost his father, and lived in his own house on Mill Road in Cambridge, a popular area with coffee and record shops. Our flirting led to Richard finally asking me out and our relationship flourished.

In 1983 he bought another house in the village of Hardwick, West of Cambridge, and asked me to move in with him. I was 21 and had been living on my own for just over two years. I was happy with my independence, but society and culture at the time pointed down the path of partnership for women like me. I ignored the niggling intuition that told me I could stay independent and looked at the logical evidence for moving in with Richard. Perhaps this was the right time to conform and be in a stable relationship, it was what people did. Most of my female friends were no longer living alone, I reasoned, and I got on well with Richard. Moving in together was what grownups did, and at 21, I'd been a grown up for some time. Despite my discomfort, I agreed to his proposal and sold my studio flat. It had doubled in price in just a few years, I sold it for £33,000. I bought my self a new car with the profit from the flat, a black Peugeot 205 GTI with a red go-faster stripes down the side. I moved in with Richard to his big house, with its big garden, contributing to the bills and food, and acted my part as half of what could have been an upwardly mobile couple in the era of yuppies and Thatcherism.

Upwardly mobile might have been my ambition, but it wasn't shared by Richard. Where I had been used to the city and the suburbs I now needed to adapt to village life and commuting to work. There wasn't much in Hardwick for young people, but we made good friends in the village despite this and spent a lot of time in the local pub, The Blue Lion, with them. It became like a second home to Richard. I wanted to progress my career and had been thinking about changing jobs. I felt restless and needed to move on, I loved my work, but knew I was capable and could do more. I also knew I was not going to get on in my career unless I had a degree. I gained my ONC and HNC in Engineering on day release at the Cambridgeshire College of Arts and Technology, which is now Anglia Ruskin.

I had just completed seven years at the Welding Institute, one year in Stress Wave emission, three years with Duncan in Ultra High Vacuum Diffusion bonding and then three years in micro joining technology with Norman Stockham as my boss. Micro joining technology involved many different methods for joining metals on a micro scale. Lasers and diffusion bonding, but one of the biggest projects was in the growing electronics industry, micro joining on silicon chips using very thin wires to bond on different parts of the silicon chip with either manual or computerised machines. Bob Clements had been working here for some years and was an ace on the manual machines, but it was my job to set up and operate the computerised equipment for different experiments I wrote the programmes that instructed the computer in this micro binding process that robotics executed. It was a forward-thinking development at the beginning of robotics, although the technology hadn't caught up with the process. The computers were huge, cupboard-sized machines that required their own air-conditioned and dust-free cleanroom, with dashboards as big as a table top. A smart phone could carry more information in the palm of your hand in the 21st century.

My skill development improved my confidence and in 1985, when I saw a technician engineer position advertised at Graseby Micro Systems, part of the Cambridge Electronics Instruments Groups, I applied for it. I was offered the job straight after interview and moved to a new engineering environment where I was working on controlling automatic wire bonding machines in micro joining technology. My situation changed from a male dominated workplace to a mixed one, I was no longer the only woman. The majority of the operators were female and I got on extremely well with the girls, and my boss, Tom Ellsiton, who was the chief engineer. In those days Tom or I would set up the automatic wire bonders for the girls to operate. I could see from a very early stage that the girls were very intelligent and could easily set them up themselves. Because I had more time than Tom, I taught them. My first pupil was Sharon who loved the new challenge and did an excellent Job. Another pupil was Tina and again she did an excellent job. The production throughput rose significantly. I didn't stop there, I taught the girls to do a lot more tasks, it made their work much more interesting and proved they were just as equal as their male counterparts. Sharon and Tina became, and still are, very good friends. Sharon asked Tina and me to be godmother to her firstborn, Georgina.

It was life-changing to work in a new place and I was very happy there, but life at home had become more difficult. It wasn't that long before I started to notice that things weren't right with Richard. We went on holiday with some friends, sharing a caravan with them at Cromer, but after an argument and a fall out, he left and went home to Hardwick, abandoning me for the rest of the week. Our good friends David and Pat were as annoyed with him as I was and took me home.

Richard developed a drinking problem and wanted to spend every spare moment at The Blue Lion pub. I didn't always go with him. At weekends I wanted to have days out by the coast, but he wanted to stay home, clean his car and go down the pub. We started to argue because of our differences. I wanted to explore and visit new places, he was happy with his routine at home. It came to a head on a weekend away with good friends who were going up to Edinburgh to watch the rugby. I agreed to go, and we hired a minibus that seated ten people to drive up there. On the day of the match the men asked, "You'll drive us home from the match won't you Helen? Then we can have a drink." Used to the company and society of men, I had presumed I'd be part of their group, the other wives and girlfriends had organised a shopping trip, and I wasn't keen to participate in that. Wounded, I reluctantly agreed, and spent four hours walking round Edinburgh on my own. I looked around the castle before I went back to the ground and picked up the group. Richard was well tanked up after the match. He tumbled into the back of the minibus and cosied up to another woman, flirting earnestly while I fumed in my role of taxi driver at the front, my hands gripping the steering wheel as we drove through crowded streets back to the hotel. We survived a meal with the others that night, I let the resentment fade, but it gnawed at me, Richard was self-contained and distant with me on the long drive home. My thoughts twisted as I worked through Monday and I rehearsed what I would say to him over and over in my mind, so by the time I got home, I was ready to challenge him, to talk about what had gone wrong at the weekend, what I felt was going wrong in our relationship. He was evasive and made ready to leave to go and see his mother for French lessons. I persisted, "Stay and talk to me now or when you get back I'll be gone." I said. He didn't take me seriously and left. After he had gone I composed myself, rang my Mum, explained what had happened and, gripping the phone close to my head, asked to stay with her. There was no pause before she answered, "Of course, you can." She said. Mum sometimes came good in a crisis. I packed up everything in my car and left. I stayed at my mother's place for a while as I searched for a new property and a new place to live. Mum and Jack were going through a rare settled spell, and were getting along a little better, so the atmosphere was not as bad as it had been, but I still needed to move out. I had just started an Open University degree and needed space to study in peace at weekends after work.

Richard rang and asked me back, but things had changed. I had seen from my mum and Jack what happened when a relationship soured, and I was determined my life would be better than that. I stuck to my guns, although it took me a while to come to terms with the break up and sort myself out. I moved into my own flat in Newmarket, at Amberley House on Bury Road. It looked out over The Gallops, the wide heath where the exercised the racehorses that would run at Newmarket. As I watched the beautiful creatures galloping ahead of each other, I had made the right decision. I moved forward as quickly as I could. I went on holiday for a while to give myself a break, and while I was away my friends and colleagues, Maurice and David Wrigley, stepped in to oversee the sale of my precious Peugeot GTI. The mortgage on my Newmarket flat was £47,000, I had to sell the car to raise a deposit. Duncan sourced an old car for £50 for me to tide me over. My work colleagues had proved their worth as friends yet again.

As soon as I was moved into my own place I pursued my BSc Open University degree in the Structure and Design of Manufacturing Systems and Electronics and bought my first Sinclair PC. Studying for the degree took over six years and involved researching modules in electronics, modelling with mathematics, living with technology and instrumentation.

My last course was Introduction to Economics, reflecting my changing role at work. There were summer schools to attend, all around the UK, my favourite place was Bath University, I went there twice. Summer schools gave me the opportunity to meet lots of good people and were hard work, but very entertaining. I had made more great friends in my workplace, like the Head of Production, David Wrigley and Head of the Prototypes department, Maurice Dunn.

I had always got along with everyone at work, sometimes I would have my tea break in the pre-fab machine shop out the back and have a chat with the blokes. I didn't discriminate between who I spent my time with or who I talked to, whether they were university educated, or educated at the school of life. I found all people interesting and worked to communicate with everyone, regardless of background. Our cleaner at Graseby was Les, he dealt with the specialist materials we needed for specific parts of the workshop. Les had some mental health issues and this different social comprehension sometimes led to him giving me inappropriate attention and presents for my birthdays. One day a big tub of acid went missing from the stores. No-one could account for it. Les had taken and hidden it, when it was finally found, and he was challenged he said, "If I can't have Helen, no-one else can." He was planning to do something terrible with the acid, whether he would have carried it out, no one knew. Les was sacked and given psychiatric help. It became a frightening time for me, I was back living on my own and worried he would find out where

I lived and turn up. But the situation did not deter me from living my life. I'm not a fearless person, but I can carry on in times of crisis. Richard continued to communicate with me too, sending me rings through the post. He wanted me back and offered to buy me a bed sofa for my flat, even though we were living apart, but I resisted.

I was coping well with work and life, but there was a niggling feeling that I could still do better, so I went for an interview with a technology group in Cambridge, who offered me a job. I mentioned it to David while I was working some overtime and he told me not to be hasty, there was going to be a management change at work, and I should wait a few days. I took his advice and held on. My main boss was being dismissed and the structure of the organisation was changing. The whole department was reorganised and I was asked to be in charge of the prototypes department as a development engineer. I would oversee all the new designs, talking to designers and making sure the designs were suitable before going into manufacture. It was a 10% pay rise. I liked the people and the place, so I said yes. I was 25 and in charge of a team of five people, it was the beginning of a managerial career that would see me promoted three more times in the next five years.

One of the most interesting projects we worked on was for CEFAS, the Centre for Environment, Fisheries and Aqua Culture Science, a government department based in Lowestoft. We designed and manufactured electronic tags for fish. Fishermen could examine the tags when they caught the fish and see the details of where to send the tag to claim their reward. It was a good incentive and a successful system, CEFAS had many tags returned and they used the information from the tag to record where the fish had swum to and how long they stayed certain areas, giving them information on breeding grounds and stock shortages.

We also made prototypes of specialist equipment for the aerospace industry, such as missiles, and the military for all sorts of equipment. At one time the whole design department became very busy and the production department needed more help too. I was promoted to assistant production manager, working with Maurice Dunn in joint charge of making sure all deadlines for orders were met. It was a big increase in responsibility and an increased salary, my production career was taking off. During the third year of my Open University Course, Alan Cousens, the head of Graseby Microsystems, asked if I would oversee production and in 1990 they made me production manager. Work had become the central tenant to my life and I loved my job. Graseby was a successful company with a turnover of about four million per annum, making about half a million profit a year. I was still working my way up, albeit rapidly. I worked every weekend, either studying for my Open University degree or at the department. I decided I needed to move out of my small flat, I couldn't sell it as Britain had just hit a recession, so I rented it out to someone who had come down from Scotland to work with us and needed somewhere to stay.

At this stage of my life I finally had some savings. Enough to put a good deposit down on a brand-new house in a cul-de-sac development, Barton's Place in Newmarket. I was the first person to buy and the first occupant of my lovely two bed at the end of the street. It had a nice bathroom, a kitchen, lounge and a garden I designed myself. My friends helped me lay the patio. As it was an end of terrace, it was the only house on the street with its own private garage. It was only a ten-minute walk to my workplace on Exning Road, which meant I could work as much as I wanted, I was always on hand and as a manager stayed late a lot of evenings.

The new development did not pan out as expected, much to my disappointment, the rest of the new builds were rented out to Americans who worked at nearby Mildenhall air base. It caused a few problems as rental properties were not kept up to the same standard as those that were privately owned. Eventually, I asked the agent to buy the house back off me, which he did, and he gave me a little extra for the work we'd done in the garden. After it was sold I bought a brand new, beautiful, three bed bungalow on Hatley Drive in Burwell, a village to the Northwest of Newmarket towards Cambridge, where I was to settle. My bungalow was my oasis near The Lode, a small river which meandered out front, so close to the house that the ducks would be my regular visitors.

At work, I was promoted to operations manager in charge of materials, engineering and production departments. I had 75 people working for me at that time, three quarters of the whole workforce of Graseby Microsystems. The industry newspaper even ran an empowerment article about me: "The company recently survived its worst ever recession, taking a 50% staff cut in which Helen came out fighting. Rising above problems of quality, lead time and costs, finding the answer in the company's sample department, where prototypes were made swiftly and efficiently by a tight knit team, Helen and her team completely revised the factory layout to bring together the main production and test teams."

The answer to the problem had seemed obvious to me, I used my communication strength to train everyone in everyone else's skills for a more equitable division of labour.

After this, the boss, Alan Cousens, asked me to do a diploma in manufacturing management, co-run by GEC and the Open University. I still had a year to do on my Open University course but put it on hold to do the diploma which was a professional qualification very much associated with my position. I found myself the only woman again in a contingent of 11 men. It meant I was spending a lot of weekends away from home, either in posh, hotel accommodation or at Dunchurch Management College. A large section of the diploma involved giving presentations. It was a bit nerve-wracking at first, as we were assessed on them, but by the time I had finished, I was near the top with my results and my confidence had soared.

9

BRIGHT SPARKS

I continued to work hard at my career and the recognition for my achievements came in the form of several high-profile awards. In 1990 I was put forward for the Young Woman Engineer of the Year award. P.J. Lester, Graseby Group Chief Executive, supported my nomination with the following statement, sounding not unlike a Victorian schoolmaster giving a report on a promising student, "Helen is that rare animal, a woman who has reached a general management position in the manufacturing industry, and at an early age!" He was a little more twentieth century in his full description, saying I had started at the bottom (true, in the machine shop making punch holes) and worked my way to the top through sheer competence. "She has a sensitivity to people, common sense and commitment to customer satisfaction."

I was a finalist in the awards and went to collect my prize at the ceremony in a neat, dark suit, with a flash of colour at my neck from a flamboyant scarf and beads. The look on my face either betrays my disappointment and competitiveness at being a finalist and not a winner, or the fact the award was given by Leon Britton who was standing next to me. Four years later I was a finalist in the Cosmopolitan Achievement Awards too.

In other work scenarios, I endured complicated economics and survived difficult times. Just after the company had endured its worst ever recession in 1993, I gave a keynote address to the Graseby Quality Conference. Despite my day to day management duties, I didn't have much experience at that time speaking in front of hundreds of people. There was a nervousness, a tightening in my chest as I waited in the wings to be introduced on the stage. I was as sweaty palmed as the night I had walked the long, dark drive to Sawston Hall with my brother as a child, but now I was a grown up, responsible and in the full glare of attention. I knew great things were expected of me. I had prepared about six prompt cards to make sure I remembered to cover all the relevant subjects. My name was announced, and I made my way up to the stage, a hundred pairs of eyes watching. I dropped all the cards. They scattered over the stage. I scrabbled to pick them up as someone shouted, "Helen will now do her speech from the floor." The audience laughed. Relieved they were on my side, I went on to give a full presentation on the theme of empowerment, which was covered by the industry periodical: "It takes guts to follow a keynote speaker like Paul Lester, who opened the Graseby Quality Conference with a thorough review of the entire Graseby group and its performance. But it also takes guts for a company to survive its worst ever recession, take a 50% staff cut and come out fighting. Operations Manager, Helen Mcmenamin of Graseby Microsystems showed how it was done, empowerment. They were faced with problems of quality, lead time and costs, and the answer was found in the company's samples department. Here prototypes were made swiftly and efficiently by a tight knit team where everyone could, and did, do everything... the improvements have been tremendous."

Things got better for the company and for me. My speech was good, I got a standing ovation and it showed how I had empowered myself to move forward.

One year, Graseby Plc organised a special occasion at one of the Cambridge Colleges, at which the renowned Cellist, Julian Lloyd Webber, gave a performance. At the bar later, the chief executive asked if I would go and see if Julian wanted to join us for a drink. I found his room, knocked on the door, he opened it wearing just his underpants. Keeping my head, and my clothes on, while others were in their pants, developed strengths in my personality which were noticed by my bosses.

In the mid-90s, Alan Cousens was asked to run another company that needed his skill and guidance. Alan asked me if I was interested in being   director and general manager for three months and if I did well the position would be offered to me permanently. I was elated, shocked, very grateful and determined to show what I could do. My first big task was to hold a meeting with one of our large customers as director and general manager. I did so well, that aged in 1994, aged 32, I was offered the position on a permanent basis. This was a very special time in my life. A massive achievement for some one that had such a difficult start. My first company car was a BMW. To me, this was incredible, and I kept pinching myself to make sure I was not dreaming.

Shortly after, I was told I would have to attend the chief executive conference in Florida. I had never been to America before, and never been on a long-haul flight. I flew over by myself. I had organised a hire car before I went, which caused me some stress, I'd not done a lot of driving on the other side of the road. I climbed in the hire car and went to start the engine. Nothing. I tried again several times before I went back to the desk and told them the car would not start. They came back to the car with me and started the car immediately. I looked so puzzled until they worked out that I didn't know I needed to put my foot on the brake to start it, it was an automatic. There were hardly any cars in the UK with this starting procedure. I drove off carefully to the wonderful hotel and met up with my group leader, Chris Fowler, who had taken his wife and children along, so they could enjoy Florida whilst we were at the conference. As we had the first day free, Chris and his family took me with them on an outing to the Kennedy Space Centre at Cape Canaveral. I was happier than I would have been at any Disneyland theme park, it was right up my street, we had a lovely day out.

My personal life had developed alongside my career and

I was becoming more settled and happier in my own place. When I was about 28 and working in Newmarket, I made one of my best female friends. Lindsay was the daughter of the quality manager, Ron Rushmore. I ran the social club for the company where I organised comedy nights, darts matches and hired it out for birthday parties. Ron told me his daughter would like to help, could I involve her? She helped on one of the comedy nights, but I didn't see her again for a while, and then in peculiar circumstances.

My mum and Jack finally split up in 1989 after her father had died and left her a lot of money. Perhaps this gave her the financial independence and the impetus to strike out on her own, but along with money from the sale of the house she shared with Jack, she was able to buy a two bedroom flat in Chesterton in Cambridge. Shortly after she moved in, she told me about her lovely neighbour who she often shared a drink with, "I've invited her for a meal tomorrow night Helen, why don't you join us, you could stay over." Mum suggested. Of course, I agreed. The following evening, I drove over and as soon as I came into the room, I recognised the lovely neighbour, it was Ron's daughter, Lindsay. We had a wonderful evening and never stopped laughing.

Lindsey persuaded me to accompany herself and two other friends, Marie and Janet, on a blind date the following weekend. I reasoned that it sounded very interesting and would probably good fun as Lindsey was such good company. The evening went very well and was definitely memorable. We met the four men in a pub in Cambridge. They were very different from my normal male associates and a bit odd. Needless to say, us girls didn't hang around long and afterwards we were doubled up with laughter over the experience. The four of us became extremely good friends and still are. I even managed to get Lindsey hooked up with my schoolmate and work colleague, Paul Evans, who she is still with today. We have remained very good friends and spent a lot of time together. Even now we have at least one weekend away together every year.

I didn't always possess a natural grace and ability within a sport. Lindsay wanted to go on a skiing holiday, I was reluctant, the thought of hurtling down a mountainside on sticks terrified me, but I wouldn't give up, I have always been willing to give new things a try. We went to have some lessons on the dry ski slope at Bassingbourn first. Lindsay fell on the unforgiving Dendix mesh, twisted and damaged her arm. This didn't deter us from going on our first skiing holiday to Norway together. We arrived and stumbled over to use the nursery slope where the children were having lessons. I was petrified of heights and hoped I could stay at low altitudes, but the very next day the instructor persuaded us to ascend the slopes with the rest of the group. I was very scared. Our instructor told us to use the gentle slopes and stop at certain points, I thought I could just about manage that. Lindsey, who was always a fearless character, made a big mistake. She went so fast down the first slope, she could not stop, and skied the whole length of the mountain, right the way to the bottom. We all remained, poised at the top, straining to make out her tiny figure so far away. Aghast and shaky I made my way delicately down the polished snow, my confidence gradually increasing until I met her at the bottom. Lindsey was still in shock over her experience and had been waiting for us for almost an hour. I was just happy I was still alive. I got much better, but never picked up the skiing bug and haven't been back since.

In 1992 I was 30 years old and the director and general manager at Graseby Microsystems. The company was going from strength to strength with rapid expansion. In 1994 we had put in an offer to purchase part of GEC Plessey, a British based international electronic, defence and communications company, who were looking to outsource their hybrid facility works. GEC Plessey had expressed an interest in divesting part of their microcircuits and our company became part of the absorbent operation in a successful acquisition that took over a year to go through.

John Smith worked for GEC Plessey in Lincoln as their operations director, running all their operations including their hybrid microsystems department that we were taking over. He visited our factory base at Newmarket in a series of meetings, accompanied by other engineers and I visited their base in Lincoln. I had not long taken over as director and general manager, so this was my first big challenge. I was always present at the meetings. John showed a lot of interest in negotiating specifically with me, he would often phone me at home to ask me questions about work. I did wonder why he kept doing that. I didn't twig that he was romantically interested in me, although I was always pleased and flattered that he called me, instead of my other colleagues. We'd developed a strong business relationship, but there was something more, we grew closer, something else was simmering.

I hadn't failed to notice what a wonderful personality John had and found myself more and more attracted to him throughout the acquisition process. We saw a lot of each other at work and gradually grew closer. I knew he was married, but he had told me he was separated, with three sons, one who had a degree and was doing voluntary work out in Zambia, one who was working at the same firm, GEC Plessey, in Oldham, and a 14-year-old living at home with his mother.

When the acquisition finally went through, John asked me if we should celebrate by going out for dinner in Lincoln, where he worked, and the company was based. I readily agreed and just the two of us went to a very upmarket restaurant where there was a bottle of champagne waiting for us at the table. A bottle of wine followed. After our meal we strolled along the River Whitham in Lincoln. It was late summer 1995, one of those evenings when the sky is velvet black and lights are reflected in the river. John took the initiative I had hoped he would take for some time and kissed me. A couple of days later I asked John if he would like to come over for dinner at my house in Newmarket. I bought in some specialist Newmarket sausages and made him sausage, mash, peas and gravy, his favourite meal. We saw each other on a regular basis, meeting whenever we could as I was still based in Newmarket and John was in Lincoln. He would travel over to Burwell and stay with me in my lovely bungalow. I had moved from being a single woman to almost co-habiting with a man, but this time, I was sure and happy about the situation.

Work was still incredibly busy, and it helped that we were both employed in similar fields, although we were separated by place. One of the most interesting projects that we had taken on from GEC Plessey in Lincoln, was the Bates Hybrid electronics which were used in the Rapier Missile System, a critical army defence weapon. When we finally manufactured them, they didn't work. Our research people discovered that the original design had an error. I was put in front of the senior GEC executives, to explain what was wrong and what we had to do to fix it. They understood and were positive about our planned fix and gave us the go-ahead. We resolved this problem within three months. That year the increased turnover from the GEC takeover was reflected in our profit. We went from a four million turnover to six million increasing our profit from half a million to a million.

Then a sea change happened in my life. After a short time together, much to my surprise, I discovered I was pregnant. John moved in permanently with me to my bungalow in Burwell. I was now sharing my life with the man I loved, no longer completely self-reliant, and about to have a child who would depend on me. At that time, John no longer wanted to work in Lincoln, so he took a better position working for an American company, Photronics, based in Manchester. He was put in charge of that base and their European companies. From Monday to Friday he was working away in Manchester, while I was pregnant and still working in Newmarket. Work were very pleased for me, there was never any question that I would leave the company. I fully intended to return to work about three months after having the baby and get a full-time nanny, so I could combine motherhood with a career.

Things don't always work out to plan, I had a difficult pregnancy, suffering from pre-eclasmia in the latter stages, which meant I had to leave work when I was seven months pregnant. I was quite ill and was admitted to the Rosie maternity hospital, part of Addenbrookes in Cambridge, to be induced. Induction can lead to a long, drawn out labour and cause distress to the mother and baby, this was becoming apparent in my case and they were just about to rush me down to theatre for a caesarean when the baby arrived. In the early stages of my pregnancy I had been convinced I was going to have a little boy, because John had had three sons, but after the 20 weeks scan I was told I was having a little girl. I was absolutely delighted. Alyxandra Claire was born on the 22nd June, 1997.

John had a couple of weeks off after the birth, but then he had to go back to Manchester for work, leaving Burwell on a Monday and coming back Wednesday or Friday. I was coping with a new born on my own for a few months and then we found a lovely nanny and I went back to work.

However, things had changed while I was on maternity leave, the company had been sold to Smiths Industries and I had new bosses. I returned to my post of director and general manger, and although the new directors were extremely good, things were not the same. After about a year I was headhunted by another company based in the new science park near Cambridge and, as had happened in the past, was offered the job straight after interview. In terms of responsibility, it was a step down from a general manager position, but they said they would change the title and offered me so much more than my current salary. It was too good an offer to decline in that day and age, so I handed my notice in at Smith's Industries. Then they changed the playing field, "No, we don't want you to go, we want you to run another company for us.: They said. This was a specialist electronics company, Application Specifics Integrated Services (ASICS). They wanted me to be managing director of this company as well and increased my salary by another £10,000 above my other offer. It was an incredible opportunity, and a substantial increase in salary, so I agreed to the new dual role. It meant a little more travelling, at least once a week to Tewksebury near Cheltenham, two and a half hours each way from home in Burwell.

During the first two years of Alyx's life, the pressure and demands of my position increased. I was doing a lot of travelling in Europe and some in America. One trip was to San Francisco to help resolve problems at another electronics company. My colleague, Steve Riches, accompanied me. I'd recognised Steve's talents and stolen him from the Welding Institute, he was especially adept at assisting with our research projects, and I knew his skills would be suited to problem solving the electronics in San Francisco.

By this time, we had another nanny, Sarah Stevens. From the first moment I met Sarah, I loved her, Alyx did too, I could see she was the right fit for us, she was there for us when we needed her and became like part of the family. She was there when I went abroad and helped balance the demands of my career and motherhood, as I had to know Alyx's childcare would be perfect while I was at work or travelling. I wanted my daughter to be looked after, never abandoned as I felt I was at times in my own childhood. Between myself, John and Sarah we made sure Alyx was loved and cared for.

Finalist Young Woman Engineer of the Year

John and I on our wedding day

Wedding picture with David and Paul

Wedding picture with our mothers

Family wedding picture

John and I on the Orient Express

12 years after our wedding day at the same venue, Quy Mill

Alyx and I

Barney, Ted and I

Ted

John and I, the best team

10

BRICK WALLS

By the end of the 90s I was a high-flying career woman with a young child, the epitome of a 'you can have it all' lifestyle. My demands were split between home and work, I was performing at speed, driving myself physically and mentally to my limits, determined to make every area of my life a success. Something had to give. About a year after Alyx was born, and at the age of 36, I started to become ill. I would suffer recurring waves of an illness with a myriad of symptoms; severe aching in my joints and an overwhelming fatigue that ambushed me unexpectedly, it felt like driving into a brick wall at 90 miles an hour. I suffered headaches and transient aschematic attacks, where I would experience unsettling periods of 'absence', night sweats, chest pain and my circulation became so poor, my hands and feet would be freezing in even the warmest weather. It was incapacitating, I could barely drag myself out of bed on the worst days and on the good days I wasn't firing on all cylinders like my normal self. From the outside, I did not look like an ill person, the nature of this illness was such that, ironically, I looked well. It was hard for people to understand how incapacitated I was. I put it down to the demands of work and being a wife and mother of a young child. Perhaps I was expecting too much of my body, but I hadn't thought I would feel like this in my late 30s, I hadn't expected to be slowing down until the sunset years of my life, and I'd planned they would be a very long way off.

I became pregnant again in 1999, suffering a miscarriage at ten weeks. Miscarriage is such a common tragedy for so many women, but barely talked about. I struggled with the levels of guilt that nagged at me as if I had done something wrong, as if it was my fault. I did not know then that the loss of the baby was probably down to my undiagnosed illness, a condition of which increases the risk of miscarriage due to clotting in the blood. I was taken into Addenbrookes hospital and had to go through the dilatate and curettage procedure, in which the womb is surgically scraped. It was a horrible, humiliating and unexpectedly physically painful time. The body responds to a later miscarriage with a state of mini labour, in a cruel mimicry of what it should be doing so many months later. There was a crash of post-pregnancy ghost hormones and delayed and unexpected waves of grief, that overtook me days and months later. When I went back to work, people were sympathetic, life goes on, but it was so difficult to deal with.

After the miscarriage, my illness recurred. I was getting vague, random and seemingly unrelated symptoms that went on for about three years. Everything seemed to be going wrong with my body. My kidney and liver were malfunctioning, I had brain issues, stomach issues and the debilitating fatigue. My GP referred me to a range of specialists, so many ologists, so many waiting rooms, tests and different hospitals. I was covered by private medical insurance through work, which gave me the ability to seek the best care, but no one could find out what was wrong with me. Everyday tasks became difficult, at times I found it difficult to drive long distances and often had to stop off and rest for half an hour. My lovely PA, Birthe, would often find me curled up, resting on the floor of my office at lunch times. One time I was in such a state of semi-consciousness she rushed me down to the doctors.

When Alyx was about four we moved to Silver Street in Burwell. A lovely house opposite Burwell House, a Victorian building converted into a residential activity centre for schools, and right near the centre of the village. It was a family house, detached, with a gravel drive and nice neighbours. Four bedrooms, one of which John could make into a study, there was a large room for Alyx and a garden with mature shrubs. Plenty of room for us to make a home. The kind of place that's settled and quiet, but still very much in the centre of the community. Alyx went to Burwell Village College school, which was just around the corner. Stress or change drove me back into the pits of my mystery illness. The stresses of moving to a new house made me ill again, the demands of work made me ill, life itself conspired to bring about my symptoms, producing an unknown adversity, that, for the first time in my life, I was struggling to overcome.

The issues with this undiagnosed illness went on for four or more years. No-one could tell me what was wrong. As soon as I was under lots of pressure at work or flying off to America, I came crashing down again, I couldn't manage. I was finally given a diagnosis of ME and signed off work for a while so in 2002, I decided to take three months off myself to fully rest and see if I could finally find out what was wrong. Work brought someone in to cover for me.

I persisted in trying to find a diagnosis. John went with me to see a sticky blood man in Rochdale and we went to see endocrinologists in Bury St. Edmunds hospital for a battery of more blood tests, they all came back negative, as they always did. The doctor there suggested that my symptoms could be psychosomatic. The implication that I was a neurotic woman and the idea that my illness was just all in my mind, sent me into an apoplexy of rage. I was inconsolable. My GP thought I could try a counsellor to help me deal with these issues and someone came out to the house. At first the counsellor spoke to John and I, then he ended with a long interview with myself. It was a hot summer's day and I was wearing shorts in an effort to keep cool. As he was at the front door, about to leave, he looked down at my bare legs. I was immediately self-conscious, I knew my legs were covered with a map of blotches and purple veins, "I hope you won't mind me mentioning this." He said, "but I've seen that before," pointing to my legs,

"I knew someone with the same skin condition on her legs and it turned out to be Lupus."

I had heard of Lupus but had ruled it out because I had had so many blood tests and it had not been picked up. John and I immediately got on the internet and googled for more information. The results were frightening, 'life limiting,' 'life threatening,' 'chronic illness.' The symptoms were exactly what I had been suffering from. We looked at who could help us if it was Lupus and the name Professor Hughes, foremost Lupus specialist in the UK came up. Armed with this information we went back to our GP and asked for a referral to St. Thomas's hospital in London where Professor Hughes was based.

We got an appointment in 2002 and that was when we first met Professor Graham Hughes, consultant rheumatologist. He had been an expert in the field for many years, developing Europe's first dedicated Lupus clinic in 1973 and discovering the clotting disorder now known as Hughes Syndrome, an antiphospholipid condition which may have been responsible for my miscarriage. Professor Hughes set up the Lupus Unit at St. Thomas's Hospital in 1985, which is now based at the London Bridge Hospital in a purpose-built centre. He listened to my symptoms and experience. Whereas before we had been met with blank faces while I tried to explain what was happening to me, here was someone who understood. He was sympathetic, he knew the symptoms were not in my head. The first test he performed was on my eyes. I'd been having a problem with eye dryness, then there was the familiar battery of blood tests. The results came back and this time they showed something. Professor Hughes told me I had Lupus.

In one way it was a relief because I finally had a diagnosis. I'd been so ill and had got to the stage where I would do anything just to be well again. Now here was a reason and a name for my condition. I was not going to die, I would get help, understanding and methods to cope with my symptoms, there was a path to recovery. I was put on medication, some blood thinners to prevent clotting and I was given tablets to dampen the immune system. Lupus is an immune system disorder where the immune system becomes overactive and attacks itself. I was taking about ten tablets a day and within a short time, I started to feel so much better, so I returned to work. All was well until the pressure built up again like a slow cooker on constant heat, until the demands of my job, travelling and long hours drove me back into illness. I had another Lupus flare up when the company sent me back to America on business and I began to realise that I couldn't cope with both work and my illness anymore. Alyx had started school and I didn't want to be ill all the time and be her invalid mother. So, I made the decision to leave. My career had been the central tenant of my life for so long, my occupation that kept me going through times of personal strife and family stress, it had provided friends who became closer than family, and I was good at it. It was an incredibly difficult decision to make, and I despaired over it. Despite my illness, my first was to keep myself busy. I have a need to be occupied, to do things for others and to be productive, that runs through my veins like iron ore in a smelt.

My friends and work colleagues gave me a tremendous send off and were very sorry to see me go. The managers came to a party John had organised at The Anchor in Burwell. I think I drowned my sorrows a bit too much. This was a period of extreme adversity, work was my raison d'être, I had to find things that would equal it in challenge and fulfilment. As a first move, I joined Alyx's PTA at school, called the Friends of Burwell Village College, and helped organise events and functions for them and did their accounts. I wanted to do more, but the illness limited my activity.

It had been a long and difficult period. It was uncharacteristic of me to not be able to do anything. Lupus had slowed my system, pouring treacle over my gears so I couldn't get out of first. I'd made plans and promises, but the illness hijacked me unexpectedly so that I had to amend and drop out of commitments. I didn't like letting people down, I wanted to remain dynamic. Lupus meant I had to re-manage and re-calibrate my whole life. Any exertion must be managed with a following period of rest, I still regularly have naps in the afternoon to manage my fatigue and keep myself in the best of health with a good diet, supplements and exercise. It's a life-changing condition.

11

WHAT DOESN'T BREAK YOU

As the years passed, my family was so important. Looking after Alyx and seeing her grow, the support of John, it meant so much to me. Our little family was at the centre of my world. My home and my garden had become the anchor that held me fast when I needed fuel to fight my illness and overcome its challenges. It was in the garden, one late summer day, while we were enjoying a glass of wine together in the warmth, that John brought out a ring and proposed to me. We had discussed marriage and decided it would be a good thing for both of us, but still, it was nice to be asked properly. Of course, I said yes. We had, and still have, as strong relationship with shared common interests like walking, cycling and travelling, nowadays in the motorhome. There is no gender division of tasks, more an intuitive sense of what needs doing before the other asks. He can be in the kitchen making a lemon meringue pie, while I'm in the garden cutting the grass. We make a good team.

The wedding required a lot of planning and gave me a

project to work on with which I was happy to be occupied. We were married on the 5th August 2005 at Quy Mill Hotel and Spa near Cambridge. It was a beautiful summer's day, Alyx was a bridesmaid, along with her cousin Ella and Harry was a pageboy. The girls were dressed in deep pink, which matched my mother's outfit and hat, and as they crowded round me in my ivory dress for the photographs, we looked like a fresh bowl of raspberries and cream. I'd chosen a strapless, satin dress from a bridal boutique in Exning and a local florist for my bouquet of old English roses in several shades of pink. Our photographs were taken in the grounds of the mill, and on anniversaries, John and I go back there to sit in the wedding bower and reflect on our special day and the life we have together. I wanted the sort of wedding that would cater for everyone's needs. We had a lot of friends with young children, as did we, Alyx was about eight years old. There needed to be something to keep them happy and occupied. After the ceremony the children had a lovely lunch in another room and a magician to entertain them, while the adults enjoyed a sumptuous sit-down meal and relaxed. In the evening we had a cèilidh band, which everyone enjoyed. It was a wonderful day that our friends still remark upon and remember as such a special occasion.

At the time, my wider family were still with me. Over the years I encouraged my Uncle John to develop an interest in photography alongside mine. He went on some lovely holidays and liked to take his camera along with him but wanted to learn how to use it properly and get the most out of it. Whenever the right photography course came up, we went along to it together, it was our shared passion. We loved each other's company and studied digital photography and landscape and movement together.

I saw my brothers David and Paul regularly. David was the closest to me in age. He was a character, inventive and playful and we were good friends always. As youngsters we were partners in crime, sneaking out at night and hiding hamsters from our mum. He was a popular lad, keen on football and a big Tottenham Hotspurs supporter, played a lot of football himself. After he met his girlfriend, Wendy, they both moved to a place in London and David went to work in a department store. Wendy got pregnant and they came back to Cambridge and set up home in a tiny flat. Wendy gave birth to their son, Joseph, and they lived as a family for a time before they split up. David stayed in constant contact with both Wendy and his son, as did I, I helped as much as I possibly could. Sometime later David met Rachel and they became a family, having two children together, Harry, who was three months younger than my own daughter, Alyx, then Ella four years later. They got married in 2005, three months after John and I were married. David had suffered illness too, he'd recovered from a liver transplant before he was married. Our family had certainly been dealt their share of adversity regarding illness and injury, in 2009 David received more than his share, he was unable to overcome the cancer that created the brain tumour that took his life. My mother was devastated. She was unable to overcome the trauma of losing a son and she died three months later, aged 73, also from a brain tumour. I helped Rachel, David's widow, and children as much as I could. I helped her buy a house near to us, so I could be on hand and take little Ella to school, looking after her until her mother got back from work at the end of the day. Harry had just started secondary school.

The loss of my brother and my beloved mother within such a short space of time brought on a severe Lupus attack, I was battling ever-present grief alongside a pervasive illness. It was only through the love of my husband and daughter, family and friends that I rediscovered my inner resilience and kept going. I missed my mother so much, I missed the lost opportunities from my childhood when she could have been a more complete mother. When I was small she was at the centre of my universe, often drifting away, sailing her ship towards a future she wanted, often alone, the crew didn't always include her children. There were times we drifted apart, but we were always connected by the strong bonds of love between a mother and a daughter. It is as if we were aware of the reflections of ourselves in each other. I can describe what she did without explaining it, I can empathise without understanding. Mum had difficulties, drifting and reconciliations, that made a collection of incidences. We remember things through the telescope of experience. Memory can lie, one person's memory of an event may not be the same as another witness. If my mother were still alive she might look on the distress I have remembering times when she was not there in my childhood, she might say it didn't happen, it was not like that. Maybe she would need to hear me say it to reignite her memory that it did.

I relied heavily on the support of my family, and on my love for animals. They had always been such an important part of my life, from the little Yorkshire Terrier, Fred, Mum bought me when we came back from holiday to the first dog John and I bought together just after we got married. A Parson Jack Russell called Barney. I had longed for a dog throughout my working life. But I lived alone and worked long hours, which meant it was impossible. Now I had more time at home, I could care for a pet again and Barney gave the unconditional love I needed to help me deal with loss and illness. He was a character. Barney was followed by Ted, another Jack Russell terrier who was only six years old when he died. I employed my love of photography to take some wonderful action shots of the dogs, some were selected for local exhibitions and one of Ted was picked out as the best in show.

When I was a child, my commitment to study gave me a space to park my unhappiness away from the tension in my mum and Jack's house. Work was a continuation of this diversion, a place to grow a new happiness, to grow a new tenacious and resilient me. The absence of work in this time of loss and illness was replaced with community involvement, in the need to do worthwhile things for others. Just as sharks keep swimming or so they die, I had to keep moving, keep occupied, be productive and contribute. I became involved with a team in the regeneration of the local village swimming pool, succeeding in our campaign to keep it open, clearing the pool, cleaning and updating it, purchasing new water play equipment. It was a job well done and started to bring in lots of new people. I developed an interest in craft as a hobby, renovating and tiling old tables, renovating furniture and glass painting. I went out and bought myself a drill and a saw for cutting wood so I could become more proficient at my crafting and I transformed the garden.

An important and gratifying job developed when I became a volunteer at a local charity, the Print Centre in Burwell. A social enterprise, training and supporting adults with learning disabilities. It was good to put my communication and newly acquired craft skills into practice and support the people working there one morning a week. I would help them to make the tea, be on reception, put cards together and place cards or letters in envelopes. This was keeping me occupied while John was at work and Alyx at school. I had always been interested in a transference of skills and appreciated the value of people, whatever their background or experience. Working at the print centre was a continuation of my work/life philosophy, bringing variety and challenge to other people's lives and it was good to work with different people. The centre supports up to ten people a day in a design studio and print shop, they have been successful in providing high quality printing and finishing services for a wide range of products. The printers love being there and enjoy each other's company.

12

PHOENIX RISING

After the accident, nearly two years on, there was that first walk out of the house with John to the local river. It was a long time before I could walk very far at all, and that walk was significant for me. It was a beautiful sunny day and I managed to reach the river, watching the dragonflies skimming the surface of the water, but I was crushed to see they were also skimming over so much litter. I asked John if he could go back with me the next day and pick it up. Of course, he agreed, team McMenanmin-Smith swung into action again. A month later I felt I was up to a slightly longer walk. Just outside Burwell village is a car park next to Devil's Dyke, one of the finest Anglo-Saxon earthworks and seven miles long. We drove out there and parked the car, but I was shocked again to see the amount of litter and a huge pile of discarded wall tiles. After a short walk, we went home, had a cuppa and then returned with our black bags and gloves. I knew how to use my phone to take photos by then, so I took some pictures, before and after our clear up. We spent about two hours doing this during which I was delighted to find a £20 note. There are always benefits to clearing up. Later that day I put the before and after pictures on the community Facebook site. The response was tremendous with so much appreciation and thanks, I also told them about the £20 note there and a few people quipped that it must be the one they had lost. There were many comments on my photographs and thoughts on the litter around the river that I had posted onto the Burwell Community Facebook page, motivated by this, I visited the Burwell Parish Council to share my concerns and Yvonne the Clerk, invited me to attend the next Parish Council meeting. There were about ten councillors at the meeting and I was given the opportunity to talk about the litter and what I would like to do to overcome the problem. I said I would like to set up a 'Litter Picking' group who would meet once a month. As Burwell is a long village we could alternate the meeting points between two places. We would need yellow tabards, litter picking sticks, black bags and the Council's help to dispose of the litter. I secured funding from the council for our equipment and we now meet monthly as a group of volunteers, the BCCC, Burwell Community Clear up Campaign, to tidy Burwell.

Every month we have up to 25 people, including children, so we are teaching the next generation to care for their environment, we have all become good friends. One autumn, the Causeway in Burwell was so covered in wet leaves, a lot of the elderly people were afraid to walk on it. I saw the fear in one ladies face one day and resolved to ask my 'Litter Picking' team if they would help me to clear it. The task was appreciated by so many people. My objection to the litter and fly tipping in Burwell, inspired two new groups in nearby villages and one in Southampton. Recently I saw a lot of litter and fly-tipped waste whilst walking in Cheddar Gorge, so I took some photographs as evidence and wrote to the local council to alert them to the problem. They were shocked and said they would send someone immediately to clear it up. Hopefully, I'm beginning to spread a national campaign! There is plenty to keep me busy, and I do need to keep busy. But also remember to be Mrs Sensible!

One of my largest and much needed tasks is helping MAGPAS. Many people do not realise they are a charity. I often give talks to groups telling them about how lucky I was that MAGPAS came to my rescue, because if they had not, I would not be alive. I've done quite a few of these, turning up at community centres and church halls, with a ready prepared PowerPoint and laptop to speak to different groups. So far, I've managed to raise £6,400 for MAGPAS through talks and a street collection in the centre of Cambridge. John and I made a big board that says, "MAGPAS air ambulance saved my life."

As well as a conversation starter it is of course, true. We raised over £300 in just that morning.

Despite the fact she was just about to sit her GCSE's when I had my accident, Alyx had inherited enough of my tenacity to keep going and sat all her exams even though her School said she could delay. She continued to study hard through her 'A' Levels, gaining the grades she needed to read Law at Exeter University. I'm so proud of my determined daughter. She has now finished her second year. If anything has been extremely good in my life it has been having such a wonderful daughter.

The other extremely good thing in my life is having such a wonderful husband. John had taken early retirement about six months before my accident. From 2006 to September 2012, he had been working with an old colleague who had an Infra-Red company in Northampton. The company was sold to an American corporation. John had stock options, so decided to take retirement. Our intention was to get full use of the motorhome and travel to France again. It was a long time after the accident before we started to use it regularly, life was so taken up with the routine of hospital appointments and rehab. The motorhome gives us the freedom to explore Britain and further afield, it means I can rest when I needed to without heading back to a hotel room and enjoy the countryside from the comfort of our own four wheels. One of the best holidays we had was a tour of Ireland and a visit to the place where my father was born. I often think that I inherited his tenacity as he never gave up and helped so many people especially his family. Thanks Dad.

My life before the accident was rich and full of challenges, life after has been even more so. I have had to re-evaluate, a brain injury is hard to come back from, my mind has re-calibrated. But, as always throughout my life, I have found ways to cope, to rise above, adapt and evolve to change. I cannot see as well, my short term memory is not good, I still have to sleep for at least an hour every afternoon. I still get Lupus attacks and I don't like driving very much, so don't go very far if I am driving. However, I'm a tenacious person, there is no way I'll give up if I want to achieve something. I hope I have used my experience to help others, to show there is a way to adapt to life through a difficult childhood, severe illness and after trauma. By writing this memoir I hopefully have shown there is always a way to face adversity and overcome it.